MW00908337

"Bob Brown is one of the most intelligent, astute, successful salespersons I have known in my 27 year career. His integrity is indisputable. He also has a quality unique among successful sales people— a strong desire to share his enormous accumulated knowledge. An expert at motivating and capti- vating people... the presentation is dynamite."

Lucille Lansing, President
Lansing Financial Group, Inc.

"At 82, he's older and a lot wiser than most of us. It pays to listen to his methods and experiences."

J.W. "Bill" Stone, President
The Mony Brokers

"Your presentation was the best I have ever seen. I'm sure that the overflow audience would agree."

Steven Riddell
Public Relations Manager
The Crossroads

"Truly one of the highlights of the conference. The group really enjoyed your presentation and the tie- ins you did with the product and sales presentations were great!"

Thomas J. Weyer
National Director of Development
Mony - Teaneck, New Jersey

"Your lecture was the highlight of our convention... great resource material. Thanks for your stimulating presentation."

Dave Jarrott, Vice President Sales
Ultimate Legal Network

"Another year, another success! Bob Brown motivates like no other speaker we have had. From the moment he hit the stage, we were enthralled with his wit and wisdom."

Harris Herman, President
Banner Software

"As a speaker, Bob is in a class by himself. Bob Brown has traveled the world as a presenter, speaking to business and social groups, inspiring attendees to reach for the top. Recognized for his charm, every presentation includes pass out material to emphasize his message. It has great take-home value."

Lassor Blumenthal
Contributing Editor
The American Salesman Magazine

"...the entertaining talk you gave at our Broker/Dealer meeting was appreciated by all. It was especially unique to have your presentation customized to include details about our real estate limited partnerships and mutual funds."

Colin M. Coyne, Vice President, Marketing
Angeles Securities

"…your ability to communicate is most impressive."

the
fine art
of
persuasion

5 secrets for making
all things possible

Robert F. Brown

Showman Publications
Sacramento, California

© 2004 by Robert F. Brown, Sacramento, California

For permission to reprint brief quotations or excerpts from The Fine Art of Persuasion by Robert F. Brown, please contact the author at:

Bob Brown
Showman Publications
1250 Norfolk Way
Sacramento, CA 95831

916-428-3210

bob@bobbrown speaks.com
www.bobbrownspeaks.com

Printed in the United States of America

Cover design and book layout by Dunn+Associates

Back cover copywriting by Susan Kendrick Writing

ISBN 0-9743726-6-8

preface

He is eighty-two years old, full of energy, a millionaire, and still selling millions of dollars worth of services to individuals and corporations. A lifetime member of the Million Dollar Round Table for forty-six years, Bob Brown is an amazing success story.

Business and selling is the greatest show on earth. Bob's background and training in the theater and on the stage give him the insight and appreciation for how the principles of showmanship that pack a theatre to standing-room-only capacity can be applied to the job of motivating people or moving products from companies to the consumer.

Bob understands the appeal that drama has to the emotions. His clever, attention-getting devices have contributed to his success when used to guide his audiences or prospects to successful conclusions. A good salesperson is not unlike a good entertainer. Successful entertainers use gimmicks, gestures, and special moves to get attention and to make themselves more recognizable. For instance, Carol Burnett always pulled on her earlobe at the end of each of her shows.

Bob has been active in contributing his time as the chairman of many projects: the Sacramento Leadership Clinic, Land of the Free radio program, the Infantile Paralysis Ball and Entertainment Show, California State Junior Chamber Speakers Contest, the Miss Sacramento Pageant, the Underprivileged Children's Summer Camp Benefit, and as Trustee of the Boy Scouts of America Council. As a leader in his community, he has been general chairman of civic projects such as U.S.O. Entertainment, Red Cross, Deaf & Dumb Association, Cub Scouts, and the Salvation Army. In recognition of assuming the responsibility of chairman of these projects, he was voted the Outstanding Young Man of the Year for community service and leadership and therefore received the Distinguished Service Award (DSA). This activity has given Bob Brown a keen insight as to the requirements necessary to become a successful leader in your community as well as your chosen career.

In his professional life, the Board of Examiners, Management Educational International, awarded Bob the diploma and title of Master of Professional Selling, the Practice of Persuasive Arts. He has qualified for Mutual of New York's (MONY's) Top Fifty Leaders list on a number of occasions, achieving No. 1 at one point. His sales have exceeded over half a billion dollars to date.

Bob continues to do what he does because he loves to help people improve their lives. Now he's willing to take some time off and share his secrets of sales success. His program is both inspirational and entertaining. You will easily see why people say, "When Bob Brown speaks...it's magic!"

Becky Bayne, 2003

table of contents

preface vii

table of contents ix

figures xi

acknowledgements xiii

part one 1

introduction 3

chapter one 7
Setting Your Sights on the Higher Goal

chapter two 27
What It Takes to Be GREAT—"Growth"

chapter three 37
Consistent Habits of the "Regular" Individual

chapter four 41
"Efficiency" for a Productive Life

chapter five 47
The Impact of "Ambition" and "Attitude"

chapter six 59
The Value of "Temperance" and "Trust"

chapter seven 63
Who Packed Your Parachute?

part two 67

introduction 69

chapter eight 71
Sales Presentation Outline

chapter nine   73
How to Say "No" to Any Request

part three   75

introduction   77

chapter ten   81
how to answer objections

chapter eleven   87
three kinds of objections

part four   101

introduction   103

chapter twelve   105
success stories

about the author   137

figures

Figure 1   8
Pie Chart

Figure 2   *11-12*
You and Your Dreams

Figure 3   *15-16*
Allen's Ten Commandments

Figures 4A and 4B   *19-21*
Magic Squares

Figure 5   *23*
What Is and What Is Not

Figure 6   *32-34*
Thirteen Ways to Stay Enthusiastic

Figure 7   *38-40*
Ten Commandments of How to Get along with People

Figure 8   *42-43*
The Bank Account

Figure 9   *45*
What Is Your Time Worth?

Figures 10A to 10E   *55-57*
Nine-Dot Challenge

acknowledgments

The Fine Art of Persuasion contains the wealth of insights that I have gained in my fifty-five years in the business world, motivating, selling, persuading, and leading. It reflects my own experiences as well as the lives and stories of people I have met in my travels around the world. Page by page, it came to life with the support and efforts of many people.

My wife, Norma, and my four sons, Rob, Steve, David, and Garrett, encouraged and motivated me from the start. Their suggestions and continually telling me to "keep on keeping on" have meant a great deal to me.

I would like to thank the people who granted me interviews as well as their suggestions, support, and encouragement. Linda Abrams, who has appeared with me at speaking engagements around the world, shared her stories of how the power of persuasion has resulted in a completely new world that she never dreamed possible. Michael Abrams, her husband and a very successful real estate developer, shared his story about "frying one egg at a time."

Arthur Banchero, who is a very successful businessman in Sacramento, California, helped me by sharing several fascinating stories about salesmanship, persuasion, and getting the job done.

Lassor A. Blumenthal invited me to New York a number of years ago to interview me for an article he wrote on 3,505 buying influences.

Peter Reveen, recognized around the world today

as the internationally renowned hypnotist and also the personal manager of the world famous magician, *Lance Burton and his Magic Show appearing at the Monte Carlo Hotel in Las Vegas*, gave helpful suggestions for developing the thrust and direction of this book.

Ted Sirlin, past president of the Professional Photographers of America, gave me continuous encouragement during this project. After reviewing the entire manuscript, he wholeheartedly endorsed the book.

I owe tremendous gratitude to Dieter Friedrich of Monte Carlo. I met Dieter many years ago in Monte Carlo. I flew to Nice, where he was regional manager of TWA. He was also the general sales agent for Ethiopian Airlines, to which TWA was giving airplanes and pilots to help start the company. As such, Dieter escorted the emperor who was invited by President Eisenhower to visit the United States and White House. The emperor made Dieter an honorary consul of Ethiopia. When the communists took over Ethiopia, Dieter resigned and moved on.

At that time he was very close to Princess Grace of Monaco, and she had appointed him vice president of her Monaco—USA Association. Princess Grace accepted his idea to start the Monaco Ambassadors Club, and Dieter still holds that position as president. This organization was developed to motivate the elite of Monaco to work together to contribute to the promotion of Monaco when traveling and to be goodwill ambassadors of Monaco when they travel to their home countries or when they are on business across the globe. Dieter is still involved in a number of activities that promote good public relations and help many organizations.

Upon meeting, Dieter immediately suggested ways I might benefit myself as well as the current business environment. He arranged for me and my business partner, Linda Abrams, to give a special presentation for Princess Grace and Prince Rainier. This was a private party in their courtyard and a most unusual and interesting session. Since then, Dieter has given me contacts all over Europe that have been very beneficial in helping me grow. I am deeply grateful for all his efforts and his energy that he has put forth on my path to success, including his input as I wrote this book.

Carol Lee, who was my first secretary, took all the loose ends I started with and put them together in a draft to help me further develop the goals of this project.

Tara Carter, who carried on the project after Carol moved on to higher levels in her career, helped me refine and add to chapters from time to time

Katie Lefevere kept the book updated throughout all the changes, especially as we neared completion.

Special thanks to Becky Bayne who took over as a general editor of this project. Becky had an enormous passion for helping me produce this book and I truly thank her for all her efforts. She suggested many ways to better convey my thoughts. Her contribution to editorial enhancement and all the changes that had been made along the way were invaluable. Her range of experience, expertise, and perception were tremendous help in bringing this book to completion. I feel very lucky.

Susan Kendrick and Graham Van Dixhorn for their writing and consulting expertise. Susan created the final flow, cohesiveness, and wordsmithing magic needed to turn the manuscript into a first-rate book.

Kathi Dunn and Ron "Hobie" Hobart created the wonderful cover design and interior pages for this book.

I feel very thankful to Lauri Thompson, who took time from her busy schedule of copyrights, contracts, and rights of publicity to share with me the story of the long journey she traveled from her first dream of practicing law to her current specialty in entertainment law.

I especially appreciate the willingness of Cynthia Kersey to allow me to use some of the examples in her outstanding book, Unstoppable. I can highly recommend her book, which has forty-five powerful stories packed with encouragement and inspiration for overcoming what may seem to be impossible odds.

Finally, I feel very thankful for the opportunity I have had to attend the many seminars of some of our nation's leaders in the fields of self-improvement, selling, leadership, and training. My earliest mentor, who worked with me very closely during the early years of my profession, was Charles Simmons of the Simmons Institute of Human Relations. By reading *Think and Grow Rich* by Napoleon Hill over and over again, I developed further steps for growth.

In recent years, the material presented by Stephen Covey, Dr. Donald Laird, Zen Kaufman, Kenneth Goode of Profitable Showmanship, Charles Roth, Elmer Wheeler, Norman Vincent Peale,

Dale Carnegie, Denis Waitley, Anthony Robbins, and Ken Blanchard have proven to be great stepping-stones in my path toward success. I feel deeply grateful for all of their shared wisdom.

part one

introduction

There are so many opportunities, rewards, pleasures, and "mountaintop" experiences available to all of us—if we just know how to make them happen. I have come to realize that the most important ingredient in this success is communication between people. If you can convey your thoughts, ideas, feelings, and goals with power and persuasion, you will create a life of true greatness.

Over the course of my career, I have sold more than a half a billion dollars in products and services —all through the power of persuasion. What I have found, however, is that the principles involved in selling products and services can be applied to improving our personal lives as well. To be persuasive, you "sell" yourself and your ideas every day. You communicate in such a way that you persuade others to your way of thinking, gain respect and loyalty, and further your most cherished dreams and goals.

What is "Selling" and "Persuasion"?

I hope that the following definitions will help the reader or student feel confident in using the definition of persuasion as a multi-purpose tool and in communicating with others.

Let's look at some definitions:

In the Dictionary:
Selling: To make acceptable, believable, or desirable by persuasion. To bring around to a favorable way of thinking. To gain acceptance or approval.

Persuasion: The act of persuading. The power or ability to persuade. A way of believing. Having the power or effect of persuading.

In the Thesaurus:
Selling: A transaction. To sell, or be in the business of stock or carry traffic of the market. Handle. Peddle. Selling ideas for self-support. To get acceptance for, win approval for, get support for. To get across or promote. Persuade of. Convince of. Talk someone into. Bring someone around to. To induce to. To win someone over.

Persuasion: Winning over, inducement, convincing, coercion, influence, opinion, conviction, school of thought, philosophy, compelling.

We all need to be persuasive in some form during our daily lives. Maybe you will need to persuade a business associate, a customer or client, your husband or wife, your children, your neighbors. We are constantly exchanging ideas back and forth. Communication, selling, and persuasion are all members of the same family. All the material in my book will help you communicate, persuade, and sell your way to your life goals by first laying the foundation of character and persistence.

You will learn not only what it takes to be persuasive, but how persuasion works, and why. People don't buy hearing aids; they buy hearing. They don't buy plane tickets; they buy fast transportation. They don't buy an easy chair; they buy comfort. They don't buy a beach umbrella; they buy shade. They don't buy a television; they buy entertainment. They don't buy life insurance; they buy peace of mind.

Someone once said that nothing happens in life or in industry until somebody sells something. It is my sincere desire that what you learn in this book will help you do exactly that so you can succeed beyond your wildest dreams in every area of your life.

chapter one

setting your sights
on the higher goal

Many of us go through life with our eyes directly on the path in front of us, at where we are right now and maybe at where we are headed. The first step toward any kind of success, therefore, is to raise your sights. Raising your sights means looking up, around, and beyond to where you would ideally like to go and who you would like to be. If you can see it, you can get there. This chapter is a general overview of the tools, personal characteristics, strategies, and habits necessary for a successful journey.

Once you have raised your sights, you need to be inspired by a driving passion to be, have, and do more. Any goal is well within reach if you are propelled by a burning desire to reach it. You need to be focused on this goal and ready to act. According to

Vince Lombardi, the legendary former coach of the Green Bay Packers, "Regardless of what you put in, everything boils down to doing the things that you do best and doing them over and over again." Here's an example of what it means to raise your sights and focus on bigger rewards. See figure 1.

Look at this pie. Seen one way, there is just one slice of pie here. Seen another way, there is all but one slice. It is simply a matter of perspective. Here's how it works. If you look at the picture from the bottom of the page to the top, there appears to be a large pie with a piece cut out of it. If you turn the picture upside down, however, and again look from the bottom of the page to the top, there appears to be only one slice of pie. By literally seeing "the bigger picture," you get a much bigger piece of the pie.

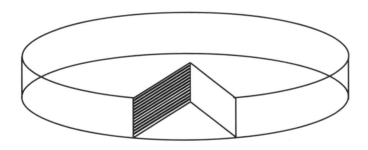

Figure 1. How you look at it.

This illustration is a simple but powerful lesson in raising your sights. What you see does dramatically affect how you act. If you see an opportunity, you are more likely to reach for it. If you don't see the opportunity, you will simply keep plodding along, unaware of the riches right in front of you and readily available for the taking.

You may ask, "Where should I go for more inspiration to help me raise my sights?" To answer this question, let's examine the characteristics that make up a great motivator and leader.

First, it is a common business statistic that companies often fail because of insufficient working capital—they end up spending more than they make. People fail for similar reasons, because of insufficient *mental* capital. They run out of ideas and fail to replace them. Creativity, innovation, and the courage to accept and even seek out change are the mandatory characteristics of any great leader.

Consider this story about a man we'll call Mr. Smith. Well equipped physically, Mr. Smith had no trouble holding his job as the caretaker of a small church until he was asked to sign some papers. "I can't write," he said, and was promptly fired. Out of a job, Mr. Smith turned to contracting and in time became a wealthy figure in the community. When he applied to the bank for a $100,000 loan, he was assured he could have it. But when asked to sign the papers, he was obligated to reply, "I can't write." The banker was astounded at Mr. Smith's accumulation of wealth and position without knowing how to write. The banker asked, "What would you have been if you'd known how to write?" Mr. Smith paused for a moment and then replied, "I would be the church caretaker."

In my own case, I find that even with the half a billion dollars of products and services that I have sold over the years, I must continually plan better, think better, and raise the bar on my acceptable standards. To achieve success, you must have direction and be persistent. The following is one of my favorite sayings:

"Press on. Nothing in the world can take the place of persistence. Talent will not; nothing is more common than unsuccessful individuals with talent. Genius will not; unrewarded genius is almost a proverb. Education will not; the world is full of educated derelicts. Persistence and determination alone are omnipotent."

Another thing successful people do is track their progress. To continue moving forward, it helps to know what you have done so far—what has worked and what hasn't. The following story of the successful experiment says it all:

A smile of triumph appeared on the face of the tired scientist. His eyes, bloodshot from lack of sleep, lit up with joy. After months of effort, his experiment was complete, assuring longer life to humans and conferring a priceless boon to humanity. Because of this phenomenal feat, the scientist was assured that his name would become immortal and that unborn millions would speak of it reverently. Turning to his secretary, he said, "Now, consult your notes and the data you recorded so that we can repeat this experiment and demonstrate again the truth that we have just discovered."

"Notes? Data?" asked the secretary. "I kept no notes or data."

If that incident had actually happened, it would be no more ridiculous than what many people do when pursuing their most cherished dreams and goals. They don't plan and they don't keep score. By this behavior and lack of order, confusion erupts. If success results, it comes in spite of poor habits, not because of good ones. We must build specific plans and keep accurate records to answer the vital questions, "Where am I going?" "How am I going to get there?" and finally, "At what point have I arrived?"

Success and happiness come when you do the things you want and have planned to do. New energy, new ideas, and new enthusiasm quickly follow. You start "hitting on all cylinders" when you know what you want and then go into action to get it!

An effective method for strategically planning and attaining your goals is to carefully consider each of the following questions and then write down your responses. Answering these questions in an honest and detailed way helps you see exactly where you stand and what you have to do to move forward. Seeing it all on paper also helps you focus and stay motivated. See figure 2.

You may already be familiar with the idea of thinking in terms of the next five years, the next five after that, and so on. Let's start planning right now! Get a pencil or pen and answer the following questions:

What do I want to happen? And WHEN?

1_____

2_____

3_____

What do I want to possess? And WHEN?

1_____
2_____
3_____

Where do I want to go? And WHEN?

1_____
2_____
3_____

How much money do I want to make? And WHEN? And HOW?

1_____
2_____
3_____

What new knowledge do I want and need? And WHEN?

1_____
2_____
3_____

What new skills do I want and need? And WHEN?

1_____
2_____
3_____

Figure 2. Plan Your Future.

There is a saying that wonderfully expresses the difference that self-organization can make: "Great men have but few hours to be great." Like the rest of us, they must rest, dress, bathe, and eat. Being human, they must make visits to the dentist, doctor, etc. What makes individuals great is their ability to plan, prioritize, and focus.

As a practitioner in *The Fine Art of Persuasion*, you have to be a jack-of-all-trades, many people rolled into one. Multi-tasking is a common phrase of the twenty-first century. Let's look at the salesperson as our model. Remember that you can apply the powerful principles and practices of sales directly to your own personal and professional life.

First, you must be a good *manager*: You must make plans for the future and keep abreast of new trends. Next, you must be the *office assistant*: You must keep records, prioritize, and manage your time effectively, following through on all necessary tasks. Eventually you will need to be a *treasurer*: You must keep an accurate record of income, expenses, and profits or, in the case of many goals, your results, efforts, and progress. Finally, you must be a *motivator*: You must be able to continually inspire yourself to move forward.

In the beginning, especially, motivating yourself can be a daunting task. You may need to find a mentor, a practitioner in *The Fine Art of Persuasion* who will support and encourage you. This individual must be trained and accomplished in your field of interest and have a sincere desire to help you succeed.

To help illustrate the effectiveness of the multi-tasking success model, let's look at the formula for failure that I refer to as, "The Five Freedoms."

Formula for Failure—The Five Freedoms

Freedom from learning

Freedom from record-keeping

Freedom from continuous planning

Freedom from responsibility

Freedom from discipline

> *Readers are leaders.*
> *Books are people in print.*
> *Learn more to earn more.*

Too many individuals unknowingly cling to these five freedoms without realizing that the immediate gratification they are experiencing is actually freedom from any kind of real success. You simply cannot be successful as long as these five freedoms are more of a priority than the necessity of carrying out the basic principles of growth and achievement.

Success is not hard. It is really quite simple. You can attain whatever you set your sights on as long as your heart, your mind, and your actions are aligned and you are willing to do things right, one day at a time, and one step at a time. See figure 3 for further inspiration.

George Allen, coach of the Los Angeles Rams, lives and works by a demanding code. He refers to his code as "Allen's Ten Commandments." While some of the code necessarily alludes to the game of football, much of what follows is certainly applicable to the game of success.

Allen's Ten Commandments

1. The greatest feeling in life is to take an ordinary job and accomplish something with it.

2. If you can accept defeat and open your pay envelope without feeling guilty, then you are stealing. You are stealing from yourself and from your employer.

3. Everyone, the manager especially, must give at least 110 percent.

4. Leisure time is that five or six hours when you sleep at night.

5. No detail is too small. No task is too small—or too big. Preparation can best be described in three words: Leave nothing undone. A winner thinks of what *has* to be done, not whether it *can* be done.

6. A loser is a man who is unprepared and doesn't know he's unprepared. A winner is a man who consciously does everything he can think of to prepare himself as completely as possible. To a winner the word "no" means "maybe" and the word "maybe" means "yes." Tenacity can be your edge, because almost everyone else will be going for the easy way.

7. You must achieve things in life. The achiever is the only individual who is truly alive. There can be no inner satisfaction in simply driving a fine

car, eating in a fine restaurant, or watching a good movie or television program. Those who think they are enjoying any of that are half dead and don't know it.

8. Nothing is impossible to those who are willing to pay the price, and paying the price is in itself an enjoyable part of winning.

9. A person without problems is dead. Everybody has problems. The successful person solves his. He is not disturbed when another day brings another kind of problem. That is exactly what he expected. He just goes to work on it. The man swayed by someone else is a two-time loser. First he hasn't believed in his own convictions, and second he is still lost.

10. Every man must play to the best of his ability. Every man is born with the ability to do something well.

Figure 3. Allen's Ten Commandments.

The average individual thinks of himself as a hard worker, but most people are really operating on less than half-power. They never get above 50 percent, although they may think of themselves as producing at 90 percent.

A man who is concerned with an eight-hour day never works that long and seldom works half that long. The same man, however, when challenged by a seventeen-hour day, will be just getting warmed up when he hits the eighth hour. Good things don't just happen to most people—you have to make them happen.

Performance is the only thing that counts. Succeeding, or winning, is the only true pleasure. Therefore, everything that is done to make winning more likely is fun.

Going Beyond Words: The Power of Dramatization

During my fifty-five years as a professional life insurance salesman, financial planner, and speaker, I have always used some type of dramatization to accentuate key points. I have discovered that audiences are more responsive to new ideas and retain them longer when these ideas are presented in an enjoyable and entertaining way. Dramatization is a powerful tool. It adds punch and gives your listeners an easy way to understand exactly what you're saying and want to say, "Yes!"

Whether you are addressing an audience of five hundred people or going one-on-one with a prospective client, there are dozens of simple ways to give any message much greater impact and get instantaneously buy-in from whomever you are talking to. The following example illustrates just how effective "going beyond words" can be. This dramatization took place at an actual murder trial:

To prove his point, a young defense attorney dramatically picked up the alleged murder gun, slowly and methodically slipped a bullet into the cylinder, and put the revolver to his head. As the jurors and trial spectators gasped in horror, the attorney pulled the trigger. But the only sound was a harmless click. Because of a faulty firing pin, the gun did not discharge. The lawyer knew beforehand that the gun would not fire, and he had rehearsed this scene countless times outside the courtroom. After this dramatization, the jury quickly delivered a verdict of "not guilty," and the defendant was acquitted. The lawyer could have asked all the weapons experts in the world to the witness stand to confirm that the gun would not fire. But all of their testimonies would not have been as effective as that lawyer's one dramatic demonstration. This example illustrates that drama and showmanship are effective ways to create a memorable impact and be persuasive in any situation.

Add this Dramatization to Your Next Meeting

Whenever you are responsible for a meeting with one or more people during a discussion of personal growth, self-improvement, leadership training, sales techniques, etc., try using the activities in figures 4A and 4B to add a little pep to the meeting.

Give your participants a copy of Magic Square #1 (Figure. 4A) and tell them that you are going to make a prediction. Ahead of time, write down the word "Self-Starter" on a piece of paper and seal it in an envelope. Then pass out the charts to each person and tell them that you have made a prediction based on their various skills. Now read the five steps in the directions out loud while each person follows along. When you are finished, each person will end up at "Self-Starter." That is the way it works out every time, but this is not immediately apparent to your participants, of course. It just seems like a very clever trick that gets every one talking and trying to crack the code.

You can then go on to tell them that being a group of self-starters means that there is obviously great opportunity for them to succeed in their lives and in their careers. Next, hand out copies of Magic Square #2 (Figure 4B). Again, read the five steps in the directions out loud while each person follows along. In the envelope for this chart, write down the word "General Manager" or whatever your goal is for the participants in your meeting, and seal that in an envelope. By following the directions, each person will end up on the square that you have marked General Manager, or whatever your choice is. After the participants have completed their charts, show them your prediction from the envelope.

Both of these Magic Squares create a lot of fun and enthusiasm that help keep the meeting light and your audience attentive to you and what you have to say. Both of these activities also reinforce the basic concept that if you follow a few simple rules, you will reap great rewards! You can elaborate on this point according to whatever predictions you make.

The Magic Squares

For instant astonishment, refer to page 20. Begin by placing your finger on any gray box. Then,

- **Move left or right to the nearest white box.**

- **Move up or down to the nearest gray box.**

- **Move diagonally to the nearest white box.**

- **Move left or right to the nearest gray box.**

Remember the description that your finger is on. Concentrate on it. That is what you will become if you simply follow a few basic rules!

Creative	Intelligent	Personable	Hard Working
Reliable	Team Player	Considerate	Self-Starter
Trust Worthy	Analytical	Energetic	Leader

Figure 4A

Account Executive	Mail Room Clerk	Elevator Operator	Sr. VP Marketing
Banquet Supervisor	President	VP Sales	General Manager
Up &Coming Astonishing Executive	File Clerk	Shoe Polisher	Supply Clerk

Figure 4B

You can also add impact to any message by creating a clear contrast in your listener's mind about what is and what isn't, what works and what does not. For example, in analyzing the differences between winners and losers, you can set up a compare-and-contrast list like the following:

Losers *wish* success would happen:
WINNERS *make* success happen.

Losers are *waiting* for their ship to come in.
WINNERS *swim* out to the ship.

WINNERS know that the ability or inability to express their thoughts, knowledge, and words is what separates successful leaders from the rest of the population.

Losers see obstacles or problems as frightful things when they fail.
WINNERS see obstacles and problems as opportunities, waiting to be solved.

For WINNERS, the word "impossible" only defines the degree of difficulty of a given problem or situation.

WINNERS know that you always miss 100 percent of the shots you *don't* take.

Losers see themselves as victims of change.
WINNERS adapt to the communications world in a fast-forward mode.

WINNERS adapt quickly to change and are victors of change.

Remember, winning isn't everything, but losing isn't anything.

Looking beyond the obvious is another way to instantly dramatize a point. Again, we usually see only what is in front of us and most obvious, not what is inside or beyond. Giving people a new way of seeing or thinking about things secures you in their mind as a leader, someone they are willing to listen to and follow. And isn't this the chief goal of persuasion? Following is a quote from Rumi that quickly and dramatically shifts the way you see the world. See figure 5.

Thirty spokes connect to the wheel's hub,
Yet it is the center hole
that makes it useful.

Clay is shaped into a vessel,
Yet, it is the emptiness within
that makes it useful.

Doors and windows are cut for a room,
Yet it is the space where there is nothing
that makes it useful.

Therefore, though advantage comes
from what is; Usefulness comes
from what is not.

—RUMI

Figure 5

Dealing with Change

The world is rapidly changing in education, knowledge, communication, and technology. Today we experience more change in a single day than took place in an entire decade of our great grandparent's lives. Consider this: A musical birthday card has more computing power than existed in the world before 1950, and every thirty seconds some technological company produces yet another innovation. For all of us, our current knowledge has a very short shelf life.

The people that prosper are those that rise to the challenge of change rather than try to resist it. We must accept the concept that what worked yesterday may not necessarily work today. Yesterday, natural resources defined power. Today, knowledge defines power. You must not "reinvent the wheel," but instead analyze the individual parts that comprise the wheel by disassembling it and reconstructing it with additional features that were absent from it previously. It is now feasible for individuals to directly take hold of the "wheel" and redefine it into something that has a large breath of potential. The possibilities are endless.

There are some people who are only interested in getting by or getting through whatever is going on around them. Others are clearly interested in getting the most out of life. The following experiment clearly distinguishes these two types of behaviors:

Crossing the River

Gather a group of people together and put them on a ferryboat. By the time the boat has left the dock, you will find that a certain portion of the people have taken the trouble to climb onto the upper deck in order to see the breathtaking scenery. The rest of the people settle indoors, thinking about what they will do when they reach the other side. We can divide these passengers into two classes: those who are interested in crossing the river, and those who are merely interested in getting across. Be a practitioner of The Fine Art of Persuasion. Set your sights on the higher goal and then enjoy everything it takes to get there.

chapter two

what It takes to be great —"growth"

To be persuasive—to get what you want and go where you want to go—requires that you possess "The Five Secrets of Greatness." If these attributes are not already part of your life, don't worry. By simply being aware of them and then learning more about them, you will start to incorporate them into your daily routines.

An easy way to remember what it takes to be great and to keep these ideas present with you at all times is to use the word "great" as an acronym, where each letter stands for one of the five attributes.

The "G" in GREAT stands for "growth." One of the distinguishing characteristics of individuals who have achieved any measure of success is their capacity for continuous growth. Growth is that life force that encompasses wisdom, understanding, personal and spiritual stature, character, and the capacity for sustained effort and self-discipline. In short, "growth" is one of the noblest words in our language and one the most significant concepts in life. Growth is something we all sense. Expressed as physical, mental, and spiritual vitality, growth is the evidence that life exists. This ability to create, evolve, and expand is available to everyone. Unfortunately, it is only accepted by a few.

Growth is part of the natural order of things. If a thing is not growing, it is dying. Growth also happens in stages. In fact, much of the growth around us, or in us, is not always readily apparent from the outside. A tree, for example, may be sending its roots ever deeper into the ground. It may be manufacturing new cells from the water, sunlight, and air. But not until it sends out new leaves in the spring do we see that it is truly alive and growing. Likewise, you, too, will have times when, from all outside appearances, you look dormant. But you are still doing the important work of growing in ways that will produce explosive results. It should be noted that the same principle applies to death and decay. From the outside, everything may look fine. But if you are not vigilant about creating and nurturing growth, you and your greatest dreams will slowly begin to die. This can be such a slow and gradual process that you may not even notice until it is too late—until there is no life force left from which to draw.

So what does it take to grow? How can you ensure an environment that supports growth? There is much evidence that individuals grow best when they have the cooperation and assistance of those around them. That is, they grow better as a member of a group than when standing alone. Similarly, even though a lone tree occasionally achieves the majesty of its full potential, it is much more common to find trees growing to great stature within groups, in groves or forests. Standing alone, the tree is more vulnerable to storms and lightning. Of greater significance, the tree that stands with others uses this competition to grow straighter and taller in its quest for space and the life-giving energy of the sun.

Similarly, the growth of an individual is least when he stands alone and is greatest when he functions as a cooperative yet competitive member of society. That individual is then aided by the natural helpfulness, guided by the knowledge and experience, and disciplined and strengthened by the competition of others.

What an individual needs most to grow is the genuine *desire* to grow. Willingness must then accompany this desire. Willingness translates into the positive qualities of philosophical reflection, orderly and determined effort, intellectual curiosity, and relentless self-discipline.

Moreover, as long as you *desire* growth and are willing to make it happen, you should set your sights on exponential growth. That is, you can grow to *survive*, or you can grow to *thrive*. Again, doing more rather than less does not require greater effort as much as it requires sheer momentum. You may, for example, need to push with all your might and weight to set a huge stone in motion. But as it starts to roll, it takes less effort to keep it going. After a while, with only the slightest pushes, you can keep the stone rolling at tremendous speed.

Now let's bring the concept of growth closer to home. Imagine one or two individuals whom you admire and respect. When you think about them, do you see the degree and consistency of their growth throughout the years. Assume that they work with determination each and every day to produce that continual growth. This is the obvious explanation for the success they have achieved and the positions of leadership they have attained. Remember, though, that to generate growth, these individuals need nothing more than the fortitude—the courage and staying power—to grow. Combining the desire to grow with the willingness to grow will create its own momentum, bringing you ever closer to your goals.

Enthusiasm facilitates growth.

Our rapidly evolving business world demands that executives be filled with anticipation, audacity, imagination, fresh insights, and initiative. Those individuals who continue to follow the rules that worked well enough in the past are too often daunted by new situations that are constantly arising in the explosive atmosphere of today's growth and change. They choose to compartmentalize themselves into groups and adopt a negative behavior known as "group think," where individuals tend to think and act according to stereotyped ideas regarding religion, race, nationality, language, custom, even television preferences. They live in prisons of their own making. Any enterprise that is to prosper must be in the hands of individually minded people.

Everyone possesses a certain amount of initiative. As an individual's circle of reference such as customs, habits, friends, laws, and institutions of our culture influence him, he remains an individual and has the power to act as an individual. We must, however, learn to think beyond our immediate environment. Our thoughts have to be projected beyond our circle of associates, both professionally and personally. Then we can expand our thinking and creativity.

The individualists who founded our nation never lost sight of the idea that in order to be an effective leader, you must continually enrich every aspect of who you are. To be a leader, you must keep growing in every way.

Who can rob a person of their individuality?
Only that person himself.

Thirteen Ways to Stay Enthusiastic

Anyone can be enthusiastic when everything is going right. But the person who can stay enthusiastic all the time is the person who will step out ahead and have plenty of "striking power" to get things done! Anyone can have this power. The word "enthusiasm" means "God in you." Here are thirteen ways to keep your enthusiasm going strong at all times:

1. Make up your mind. Things happen only when you make a decision and then act on it.

2. Don't save enthusiasm for special occasions; every day is special.

3. Be on the hunt for new ideas. Expose yourself to new ideas and learn from them by reading, trying a new approach, taking a course, exploring, and experimenting. You never know where your next big idea will come from.

4. Hear your own voice. Does it *sound* enthusiastic? Not only what you say but how you say it can have a huge impact on you and those around you. Make your voice your ally. Become aware of its power.

5. Associate with enthusiastic people. Make a list of them now.

6. Add variety to your life. This extends to what you think about, places you go, hobbies, work around the house, physical activity,

and more. Variety will keep you growing, interested, *and* interesting.

7. Make a definite plan. Create a scene in your mind—something you would like to do, happen, or become. Think about it. Write it down. Carry it in your pocket. Talk about it to positive people only. Now do one thing to start making it happen.

8. Put a high value on YOU. Think highly of yourself. Use this phrase to help you: "I am just as good as the other person...but no better!"

9. Buy and wear good clothes—you are worth it. One good-quality suit is worth more than three poor-quality suits. A good outfit makes you walk better, feel better, and carry yourself with confidence and poise. When you feel enthusiastic, others see you that way, too.

10. Do one thing at a time. You can do many things in a day —but one at a time. Focus on and do each one well.

11. Have strong feelings. Don't always say, "I don't know." Know what you feel most strongly about—and why!

12. Give people a reason to like you. Generously support others with appreciation and praise. Make them believe in themselves, and therefore in you. As a general rule, talk 10 percent of the time and listen 90 percent of the time.

> Go deep into people's hearts; they will love and admire you for it and this will in turn fuel your own enthusiasm.
>
> 13. Believe in God, the Divine, or whatever you call on for spiritual support. This is the greatest secret for sustained power in your daily life. Your faith will make you a better man or woman...a better mother or father...a more powerful executive...a more consistent producer. It will give you genuine peace of mind, and that, too, is power!

Figure 6

The Million Dollar Round Table (MDRT) is the premier association for the world's best sales professionals in the life-insurance-based financial services business. MDRT provides its members with resources to improve their technical knowledge, sales, and client service while maintaining a culture of high ethical standards. Round Table membership is an exclusive honor that is achieved only by a small percentage of all life insurance and financial service advisors worldwide. MDRT is composed of more than 23,000 qualifiers who reside in sixty-six nations and territories, representing about 475 companies.

I can recall my personal desires to qualify for MDRT when I began my career in the life insurance industry, and then raising my sights to the life membership level with annual qualification thereafter as a continuing goal. Currently, as a life member of the MDRT for the past forty-six years, I have discovered that in order to achieve success, one must have both enthusiasm and direction. Clear objectives are vital to obtain any desired goal in life. To be recognized in the life insurance profession, it is vital as well as rewarding to achieve the title of MDRT. Once you qualify for MDRT or other elite organization in your industry, your potential to achieve even greater goals increases dramatically. Enthusiasm thus facilitates constant growth.

chapter three

consistent habits of the "regular" individual

The "R" in GREAT stands for "regular" individual. Consistent productivity and service, humble in the right degree, receptive to other viewpoints and suggestions—these are all attributes of the truly successful individual. In other words, to be great you must first be good. You must be genuine and possess a sincere desire to achieve your goals and help others achieve theirs. You want to put yourself neither above anybody else nor below. This is how to gain the respect you want from the people around you. This is the place where persuasion begins.

A prime example of this quality of the "regular" individual is Charles Schwab, the magnate who established the Bethlehem Steel Company. His tact and his charisma helped pave the way toward his successful career. One day, for instance, while Schwab was walking through a section of the plant where smoking was prohibited, he noticed that three men were smoking cigarettes. He reached into his pocket, pulled out three cigars and said, "Boys, have a cigar on me, but I would appreciate it if you would smoke them outside." There were no further violations after that point.

In addition, if you stand for good by helping others, such as being active in humanitarian work, then your voice can be a powerful influence. With all the demands on our time and energy, it is easy to become complacent about participating in community projects and services. But we need to raise our sights in this endeavor as well to be great motivators and leaders. See figure 7.

The Ten Commandments of How to Get along with People

1. Keep skid chains on your tongue. Always say less than you think. Cultivate a low, persuasive voice. How you say it often counts more than what you say.

2. Make promises sparingly and keep them faithfully, no matter what it costs you.

3. Never let an opportunity pass to say a kind and encouraging word to or about somebody.

Praise good work done, regardless of who
did it. If criticism is needed,
criticize helpfully, never spitefully.

4. Be interested in other people—their pursuits,
well-being, homes, and families. Celebrate
with those who rejoice. Weep with those who
weep. Let everyone you meet, however humble, feel that you regard them as important.

5. Be cheerful and enthusiastic. Keep the corners
of your mouth turned up. Hide your pains,
worries, and disappointments under a smile.
Laugh at good stories and learn to tell them.

6. Keep an open mind on all debatable questions. Discuss, but do not argue. It is a mark
of superior minds to disagree and yet be
friendly.

7. Let your virtues speak for themselves and refuse
to talk of other people's vices. Discourage gos-
sip. Make it a rule to say nothing about someone unless it is something good.

8. Be careful of other people's feelings. Wit and
humor at someone else's expense are rarely
worth the effort and may hurt where least
expected.

9. Pay no attention to ill-natured remarks about
you. Simply believe that nobody will believe
them. Remember that what someone says
about you reflects more on them than it does
on you.

10. Don't be anxious. Do your work, be patient, and keep a gentle disposition. Forget self and you will be rewarded.

Figure 7

chapter **four**

"efficiency"
for a productive life

The "E" in GREAT stands for "efficiency." The essence of efficiency can best be presented through the countless accomplishments of Thomas Jefferson. His accomplishments offer a lesson to people who say, even in these days of labor-saving devices, "I just don't have time." The following are just a few of Jefferson's incredible accomplishments:

He graduated from college in less than three years. Soon thereafter, he studied law and was admitted to the bar by age twenty-four.

He invented the plow, letter-copy press, double swinging doors, seven-day calendar clock, and countless other gadgets that we all still benefit from today.

He established the decimal system for U.S. currency.

He served as a member of his state legislature,

governor, minister to France, secretary of state, vice president, and served two terms as the third president of the United States.

He fought for a system of government that made the U.S. a democratic republic, not one ruled by the aristocracy.

From this example, and from what we witness in the life of anyone we respect for what they have accomplished, efficiency is making the best use of your time and effort. If you look closely, you will see that it is also a matter of establishing priorities. Don't fritter away your time with dozens of daily distractions. Set your sights on what you want and determine what steps will take you there. Concentrate your time and efforts on those steps and you, too, will accomplish so much more of what if truly important to you. See figure 8.

The Bank Account

Imagine that there is a bank that credits your account each morning with $86,400. It carries over no balance from day to day. Every evening it deletes whatever part of the balance that you failed to use that day. What would you do? Draw out every cent, of course! Each of us has such a bank. It is called "time." Every morning it credits you with 86,400 seconds. It carries over no balance. It allows no overdrafts. Each day it opens a new account for you.

The Clock Is Running.
Make the Most of Today.

To realize the value of one year,
  ask the student who failed a grade.
To realize the value of one month,
  ask the mother who gave birth to a premature baby.
To realize the value of one week,
  ask the editor of a weekly newspaper.
To realize the value of one hour,
  ask the lovers who are waiting to meet.
To realize the value of one second,
  ask the person who just avoided an accident.
To realize the value of one millisecond,
  ask the person who just won a silver medal
  in the Olympics.

Figure 8

Treasure every moment you have. In addition, treasure it more by sharing it with someone special. Friendship is a rare jewel. Friends make you smile and encourage you to succeed. They lend an ear and share words of praise. Real friends always open their hearts to you. Remember that time waits for no one. Yesterday is history. Tomorrow is a mystery. Today is a gift, that is why it is called "the present."

The impact procrastination has on our daily lives is stupendous. It's the "thief of time" that often deprives us of satisfaction, success, and happiness. Procrastination can cripple any aspect of your life. In business, for example, there are always deadlines to meet. Making the effort to continually meet these deadlines efficiently and productively cements your reputation for excellence and generates endless opportunities. Postponing or even missing deadlines may seem justifiable at the time. But little by little this sort of procrastination erodes your reputation, and opportunities for profit and fulfillment begin to disappear.

Without a doubt, procrastination is a menace to success. Today's businesspeople at the height of their success have tackled the issues that were necessary for their advancement. It doesn't take monumental efforts to succeed. It is simply the steadfast attention to the smallest details along the way that add up to the big successes. Keeping your eye on tomorrow's opportunities and rewards motivates you to take care of today's business.

There is a difference between work and intelligent work. All professionals need to display a degree of intelligence so that they are able to accomplish a maximum efficiency and effectiveness during their workday. In the sense that one is encouraged to work intelligently, one is also urged to play intelligently. It is no less important to organize one's work than it is to organize ones' recreation. To see the real impact of both efficiency and procrastination, see figure 9.

What's Your Time Worth?

If You Earn	Every Minute Is Worth	Every Hour Is Worth	In a Year One Hour a Day Is Worth
$ 2,000	$.0170	$ 1.02	$250
2,500	.0213	1.28	312
3,000	.0256	1.54	375
3,500	.0300	1.79	437
4,000	.0341	2.05	500
5,000	.0426	2.56	625
6,000	.0513	3.07	750
7,000	.0598	3.59	875
7,500	.0640	3.84	937
8,000	.0683	4.10	1,000
8,500	.0726	4.35	1,063
10,000	.0852	5.12	1,250
12,000	.1025	6.15	1,500
14,000	.1195	7.17	1,750
16,000	.1366	8.20	2,000
20,000	.1708	10.25	2,500
25,000	.2135	12.81	3,125
30,000	.2561	15.37	3,750
35,000	.2988	17.93	4,375
40,000	.3415	20.49	5,000
50,000	.4269	25.61	6,250
75,000	.6403	38.42	9,375
100,000	.8523	51.23	12,500

Figure 9

This is based on 244 eight-hour working days in a year. In other words, the average salesman or executive might spend as much as $2,500.00 in lost time for an extra cup of coffee at one cup per day, for the 244 days.

Start to prioritize your objectives by writing them down. You will be able to clearly focus on your goals and accomplish all that you had ultimately intended to do. Goals are measurable—the more definitive your goals, the easier it is to track your progress. Be accountable to your goals. Watch yourself closely to see that you are doing at least one thing every day to bring you closer to achieving your goal. Keep your personal goals and deadlines highly visible so that you will be motivated. Keep reminders on your desk, by your phone, in your briefcase or purse. Goals must be a personal decision, because no one else can impose them on you or accomplish them for you.

The efficient individual recognizes the need to eliminate procrastination from his or her life.

chapter five

the impact of "ambition" and "attitude"

The "A" in GREAT stands for "ambition" and "attitude." Ambition is desire, wanting to be the best motivator, leader, executive—whatever it is that you have set your sights on. It includes having definite goals in life, driving stakes into the future, possessing optimism throughout the day, and striving to be a respected authority figure in your field. Attitude is your mental position and emotional response to life. Make every effort to be sincere, giving, and helpful. These simple, yet often overlooked traits, are the cornerstones for success in any situation. Think always of how you can reach out to others, even in small ways, and you will enjoy countless rewards.

You can combine ambition—your desires and goals—and attitude—your genuine generosity—in countless ways. The most successful people make it a point to pass along articles, book reviews, and other items of interest to clients, co-workers, or supervisors. A new book on the art of cross-examination, for example, could be sent to the client who is a trial lawyer and interested in that topic. You could pass along articles or books on sports, entertainment, art, and architecture to clients who would have an interest in those topics. Another way to develop connections with individuals you ultimately want to influence is to be aware of current events that relate either directly or indirectly to their area of business, expertise, or interest. Be an information hound. Search the Internet. Read newspapers and a wide variety of magazines. You can then pass along what you find by email, fax, telephone, or in person the next time you meet.

An incredible example of how to cater to the needs and desires of those you want to impress is in force every day at the Oriental Hotel in Bangkok. This fine hotel attracts a very influential group of guests from around the world. Whenever a guest checks in, the hotel keeps a record of all preferences: food, wine, room service requests, etc. The hotel staff refers to these activities as its "Secret Service." This information is filed until the next visit, when the guest will find that his or her every need has already been looked after so that they can enjoy a completely customized and pampered stay. In this way, the hotel creates very loyal customers.

For example, one night a certain guest ordered dinner. As usual, the staff kept a record of all the food and wine the guest ordered. Later in the week, the guest said he wanted to travel to one of the hotels sister locations, across the river. So the staff immediately contacted the other hotel and related all the information they had on this guest. When the guest arrived, he was very pleased and surprised that the hotel had taken such good care of him.

Paying attention to even the smallest personal details—interests, likes and dislikes, birthdays, anniversaries, etc.—can help you make a profound impression on almost anyone. This is the foundation of persuasion, creating loyal connections with those who can help you reach your goals. Do make sure, however, that you combine this kind of ambition with the *right* attitude. Cultivate a genuine desire to serve. Create a habit of attention, giving, and generosity—those "random acts of kindness"—for their own sake as well as for what rewards you may reap. In doing so, you grow not only your sphere of influence but also your very character.

Consider this quote from Vincent B. Coffin, long recognized as a champion of education: "Whenever you have a generous impulse, follow it." Although this may not come naturally at first, done often enough, it will become a habit. Successful individuals in every line of work practice generosity with regularity and grace. According to Santayana, the great literary philosopher, performing these services creates equality, the basis of friendship itself.

The largest room in the world is the room for self-improvement!

The following advertisement describes the characteristics of ambition from all aspects:

Wanted:

An individual for hard work and rapid promotion.

An individual who can find things to be done without assistance.

An individual who gets to work on time, and does not imperil the lives of others in an effort to be first out of the office at night.

An individual who does not sulk about an hour's overtime in emergencies.

An individual who listens carefully when spoken to and asks only enough questions to ensure the accuracy of carrying out the instructions.

An individual who responds quickly, making as little noise as possible when doing so.

An individual who looks you straight in the eye and tells you the truth every time.

An individual who does not pity himself or herself for having to work.

Apply Anywhere: The world is searching for such individuals!

Attitude is summarized in the following essay by author Charles Swindol:

Attitude

"The longer I live, the more I realize the impact of attitude on life. Attitude to me is more important than facts. It is more important than the past, than education, than money, than circumstances, than failures, than success, than what other people think, say, or do. It is more important than appearance, giftedness, or skill. It will make or break a company as well as a home. The remarkable thing is we have a choice every day regarding the attitude we will embrace for that day. We cannot change our past, nor can we change the inevitable. The only thing we can do is play on the one string we have, and that is our attitude. I am convinced that life is 10 percent what happens to me and 90 percent how I react to it. And so it is with you. We are in charge of our attitudes."

The impact of attitude is also be expressed in this poem by Dr. Leo Buscaglia:

Remember the day I borrowed your brand new car and I dented it? I thought you'd kill me, but you didn't;

And remember the time I dragged you to the beach and you said it would rain and it did? I thought you'd say I told you so, but you didn't;

And remember the time I flirted with all the guys just to make you jealous and you were? I thought you'd leave me but you didn't;

*And remember the time I spilled blueberry pie
all over your brand new car rug? I thought
you'd smack me but you didn't;*

*And the time I forgot to tell you that the dance
was formal, and you showed up in jeans? I
thought you'd leave me forever, but you didn't;*

*Yes there are lots of things you didn't do, but
you put up with me and you loved me and you
protected me. And there were lots of things I
wanted to make up to you when
you got back from Vietnam, but you didn't.*

One of the most important elements of success, in any area of life, is a positive attitude. The desire to serve a useful purpose in life is one of the most deeply rooted human instincts. The achievement of this objective in reasonable measure is one of the most satisfying experiences you can have. These moral and social purposes help distinguish certain individuals from all others. Unless an individual feels that his work has importance and usefulness to others, he becomes frustrated, despondent, and thus, ineffective.

Through observation, it is apparent that another common trait among most successful people is an attitude of optimism in every aspect of their lives. Optimists see opportunities in difficulties, while pessimists find difficulties in opportunities. In my opinion, the important thing is to keep your eye on the doughnut instead of the hole. A positive mental attitude is thus a priceless ingredient that can carry even mediocre ability to phenomenal heights of accomplishment. It is the magnet that attracts success.

The third most imperative attitude is that of confidence, belief in yourself and your abilities. People tend to regard you as you regard yourself. Speak with confidence, and others will respect you. Act with confidence, and others will follow you. Be sure, however, that your confidence is backed up by a genuine knowledge, skill, and commitment. Doing so will ensure that the trust others place in you will deepen over time as you continually prove yourself to be worthy of their confidence as well as your own.

Success does not come automatically just by possessing these various attitudes. Success is also dependent on making the necessary sacrifices in time and effort to reach your goals. But any effort to incorporate these attitudes into your life will make the difference between an average outcome and extraordinary success.

Expand Your Thinking

Self-motivation and expanding our thinking require that we learn to think *and* act "outside the box." We have to gather fresh ideas, search out other people's ideas, view relationships, keep the bigger picture in mind. We do this through reading, studying, and all forms of communication.The following description from wealth advisor John Childers is an example of how people get stuck in whatever their "box" is: "If you're an average person, you don't get rich in this world, do you? Haven't you been told all your life that average people get average jobs, marry other average people, and lead fairly average lives? Then average people have average children, and the cycle continues. "Look at what happens to most people in their lives and you're likely to discover that many of them tend to remain in or near the economic level into which they were born. If you were born into an economically deprived family or an abusive family or a dysfunctional family or even an average family, it's not easy to break out. Every day you live with some kind of deprivation, abuse, craziness, or mediocrity. "Fortunately for you…you can change the way your life turns out, if you're just willing to make a few changes.

Test the expansiveness of your thinking right now with the Nine-Dot Challenge. See Figure 10A.

Here is the challenge. Take a pencil and draw four straight lines that will connect all the dots on the page. Once you draw a line from one dot to the next you cannot go back over that line again. You simply draw your next straight line to connect as many of the dots as possible with that line. If, after you have drawn your four straight lines, you have connected all the dots, then you have succeeded. This is not easy and most people do not succeed without some help. If you do it the first time, you should be congratulated. If it takes more effort or you have to refer to the instructions, that's OK. Either way you are experiencing a whole new way of stretching your mind and expanding your thinking.

Good luck and I wish you success!

The object is to connect all the dots on this page, using only four straight lines. Once you put your pencil on the paper to drawn a line, you may not lift it. There can be no curves or circles, and you cannot draw over any lines that have already been drawn.

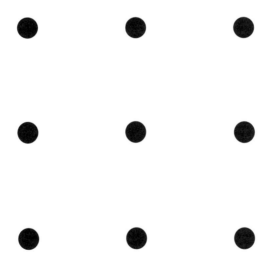

Figure 10 A

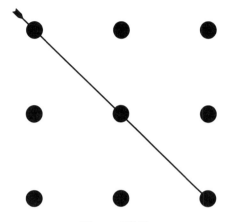

Figure 10 B

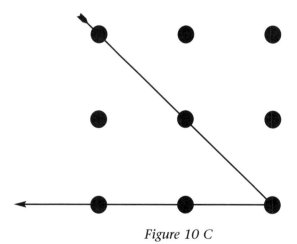

Figure 10 C

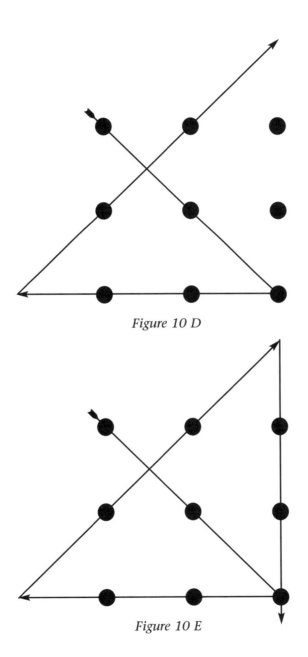

Figure 10 D

Figure 10 E

chapter **six**

the value of
"temperance"
and "trust"

he "T" in GREAT stands for "temperance" and "trust." In the context of success, temperance can be looked at as taking the long-range view. It is so tempting to feel satisfied with the first signs of success, to revel in the thrill of immediate gains, to be satisfied with instant gratification. But keep in mind that the bigger your goals and the higher you have set your sights, the longer it may reach the fullness of success. Trust that your confidence, skills, enthusiasm, ambition, and attitudes will take you there. Of course, every accomplishment along the way is cause for celebration. But always keep your desires set on the goals and rewards you can attain if you keep moving forward.

Temperance is also the quality of patience, with yourself and with others. Enjoy the path and the process. Be receptive to the viewpoints of others. Pay attention to and incorporate all that you learn along the way.

Here then, is what it takes to be GREAT: continuous growth, being a regular individual, efficiency, developing your ambitions with a positive attitude of optimism and confidence, temperance in the achievement of your goals along with trust that you will reach them.

Doing what it takes to be GREAT translates into the birth of a triumphant leader. Think of it this way:

> If you work with your hands,
>   you are a laborer.
>
> If you work with your hands and your head,
>   you are a craftsman.
>
> If your hands, head, and heart are required,
>   you are an artist.
>
> But if it takes hands, head, heart, and feet,
>   then you are a leader
>   —a practitioner in *The Fine Art of Persuasion.*

When one works hard, thinks clearly and objectively, performs honestly and with a steadfastness of purpose, then all these elements become important beyond their intended purpose. Along with them comes the ability and influence to do well, help others, and carry associates to greater accomplishments, security, and happiness. The satisfaction of doing for others—isn't that one of life's richest rewards?

This philosophy is reflected in the following poem:

We Learn What We Live

If we live with criticism, we learn to condemn.

If we live with hostility, we learn to fight.

If we live with ridicule, we learn to be shy.

If we live with jealousy, we learn to feel guilty.

If we live with encouragement, we learn confidence.

If we live with praise, we learn to appreciate.

If we live with fairness, we learn justice.

If we live with security, we learn to have faith.

If we live with approval, we learn to like ourselves.

If we live with acceptance and friendship, we learn to find love in the world.

> *Only one thing is more important than learning from experience, and that is not learning from experience.*

Follow the great motivators themselves for more inspiration and instruction:

The Magic of Believing by Claude Bristol
Showmanship by Zen Kaufman
Think and Grow Rich by Napoleon Hill

chapter seven

who packed your parachute?

C harles Plumb, a U.S. Naval Academy graduate, was a jet pilot in Vietnam. After seventy-five combat missions, his plane was destroyed by a surface-to-air missile. Plumb ejected and parachuted into enemy hands. He was captured and spent six years in a Communist Vietnamese prison. He survived the ordeal and now lectures on lessons learned from that experience.

One day, when Plumb and his wife were sitting in a restaurant, a man at another table came up and said, "You're Plumb! You flew jet fighters in Vietnam from the aircraft carrier Kitty Hawk. You were shot down!"

"How in the world did you know that?" asked Plumb.

"I packed your parachute," the man replied.

Plumb gasped in surprise and gratitude.

The man pumped his hand and said, "I guess it worked!"

Plumb assured him, "It sure did. If the parachute hadn't worked, I wouldn't be here today." Plumb couldn't sleep that night, thinking about that man. He says, "I kept wondering what he might have looked like in a Navy uniform: a white hat, a bib in the back, all bell-bottom trousers. I wonder how many times I might have seen him and not even said, 'Good morning, how are you?' or anything because, you see, I was a fighter pilot and he was just a sailor."

Plumb thought of the many hours that sailor had spent at a long wooden table in the bowels of the ship, carefully weaving the shrouds and folding the silks of each parachute, holding, in his hands each time the fate of someone he didn't know.

Now, Plumb asks his audience, "Who's packing your parachute?"

Everyone has someone who helps provide what it takes to make it through the day.

Plumb points out that he needed many kinds of parachutes when his plane was shot down over enemy territory. He needed his physical parachute, of course, but also his mental parachute, his emotional parachute, and his spiritual parachute. He called on all these supports before reaching safety.

Sometimes in the daily challenges that life gives us, we miss what is really important. We may fail to say "hello," "please," or "thank you." We may fail to congratulate someone on something wonderful that has happened to them, give a compliment, or just do something nice for no reason.

As you go through this week, this month, this year, recognize the people who pack your parachute.

> *Who you are with,*
> *is who you will become.*

part two

introduction

What are you selling? In the Introduction to Part One, I described how each of us is engaged in sales every day. There are countless situations where you must promote your ideas, win acceptance and support, bring someone around to your way of thinking. You will need not only to persuade others, but yourself as well. Whether or not you have thought about it this way, this *is* the essence of sales. It is the foundation of persuasion. It is what each of us needs to reach our goals and turn our dreams into reality.

You also now understand that much of what you need to be GREAT is achieved by developing good character, habits, and attitudes. This is the fertile ground in which success takes root and thrives. It is the foundation upon which you build your skills in persuasion. I said in the beginning of this book that I have gained much of my own career success through the power of selling and that the wisdom I have to share can be used in any area of life—in any of the "selling" you do.

Now, in Part Two, I will show you how these insights, techniques, and tools play out in professional sales situations. Because my expertise is in selling life insurance, I will be using that as my model. You can then apply what you learn to your own everyday "sales" situations. Remember, that selling, persuading, and *getting* what you want involves a large measure of *giving* what is required, both of yourself and to others.

If you're ready, it's time to watch carefully and

listen closely. What you are about to learn are the same principles that I have used to sell more than a half a billion dollars' worth of products and services throughout my career. Just imagine what they can do for you!

chapter eight

sales presentation
outline

In 1948, I enrolled in one of the first self-improvement courses I ever took. The speaker passed along a very simple communications formula that I have now used successfully for more than fifty years. That something so simple could be so effective is still amazing to me. That it has stood the test of time is even more incredible. The following outline is will help you in any presentation you give, article you write, or idea you want to promote. Use it anytime you must communicate clearly, succinctly, and effectively to get your point across and make an immediate impact. You can easily adapt this outline to any situation.

It goes as follows:

Surefire Sales Formula

What's that?
What I mean is…
For example…
So what?

First, you tell your listeners exactly what you are going to tell them. This immediately gets their attention and tells them what to expect. It must capture their attention immediately. Next, you expand on this opening statement. You enlarge the idea by putting it a different way. You then give an example to show how the idea works. This is the main body of your message. You can use stories, jokes, your own experiences—whatever makes the idea come alive and gives it credibility. Finally, you close by telling your listeners why this matters to them and what they will get out of it. If you follow this format, you have your complete presentation, article, etc. With your listeners now on your side, you wrap up with a story or joke to keep the enthusiasm high, then you ask for their support, their consent to a decision —whatever it is you want to accomplish.

Failing to prepare is preparing to fail.

chapter nine

how to say "no" to any request

While we are on the subject of persuading —asking for support of various kinds—it is equally important to know how to define and protect our own boundaries when we are on the other end of a request.

Over the years I have been asked repeatedly to participate in various committees, projects, and meetings. Usually I try to say yes and be of service whenever possible. But there are times that other personal or professional commitments make it impossible to accept a new request. I know that with the load and responsibilities I already have, I would not be able to take on something new and do a satisfactory job. So the question is, how to say no. Sometimes this is embarrassing because the request may be from a personal friend, a close business associate, or someone

I would ordinarily want to or be obligated to help.

I have found that the following approach is a lifesaver in these situations. When presented with a request, I will say, "You are doing a fine job. Please continue on with it while I make my decision." This does three things: It relieves the immediate pressure and buys you some time to consider their request; it gives you a way to support the person simply by encouraging them; and it may, in fact, do so to the extent that the person can go on without any further assistance from you. If a more definite reply is still needed, I will then say, "I am sorry, but at this particular time I am going to have to say no. This is for personal reasons. I'm sure you understand." That's it—no lengthy explanations, just a simple "no." Most people will not press further.

In most situations we put more pressure on ourselves than we realize. We are the ones who feel bad for saying no, not the person who asked us. Know your boundaries and live by them. Most people will respect you even more for it.

part three

introduction

We will now continue to use the sales model to demonstrate the best techniques of persuasion. Part Three, therefore, addresses objections and what to do when someone says no. An effective, field-tested plan is a must. Again, the following chapters focus specifically on examples from the arena of professional sales. You can easily adapt what you learn to just about any situation you encounter.

Almost from the first day I entered the life insurance business more than fifty years ago, I have steadfastly believed that we have been tackling the problem of handling objections the hard way. True, many earnest life insurance underwriters have vigorously explored the subject, and much of their findings have been published. But in contrast to other steps in the sales process, where a rather wide variety of effective techniques are available, only rarely has anyone presented a new approach to the art of meeting objections. About all we have to work with are the following:

A breakdown, or classification, of objections.

A series of suggested stock answers to be memorized.

The stock answers that we have used for so long assume that the salesperson will encounter a standard set of conditions or circumstances. The age, education, and degree of intelligence of the person raising the objection are seldom taken into account, nor are the factors of time and place.

For example, the parents of two sons, ages eight and eighteen, faced with the problem of answering their youngsters' petulant objections to rules for nights out or the amount of weekly allowance would not present the identical explanations and counter-arguments to both boys. Yet many salespeople, in answering objections to the purchase of life insurance, have relied on the stock-answer method, which all too often leads to confusion, uncertainty, and ineffectiveness in closing the sale.

Many agents have the false belief that they can satisfactorily overcome objections by means of some stereotyped, memorized trick. Eventually, however, the thoughtful agent discovers that complete confidence in dealing with objections, plus increased effectiveness in closing, comes from recognizing that every honest objection is really a symptom or clue to the *real* cause of the objection. That is, any objection is just a sign that the prospect may simply need and expect a better reason to buy—a reason that conveys the greatest benefit to *them*.

"You will never make the cover of Vogue because you don't have blond hair and blue eyes."

This was a remark make to Cher by photographer Richard Avedon.

When Cher did appear on the cover of Vogue, the magazine sold more copies than it had ever sold before.

Objections, then, should be welcomed, not dreaded. They disclose the prospect's symptoms, which you must know to correctly diagnosis the real cause of the prospect's resistance. Knowing the cause, we then can prescribe a treatment aimed directly at this cause and not at the symptoms.

Like the physician, the agent must recognize the symptoms in order to make a correct diagnosis. Once the correct diagnosis has been made, the most effective treatment will suggest itself almost automatically.

Objections, then, should be welcomed, not dreaded. They disclose the prospect's symptoms, which you must know to correctly diagnose the real cause of the prospect's resistance. Knowing the cause, we then can prescribe a treatment aimed directly at the cause and not the symptoms.

Like the physician, the agent must recognize the symptoms in order to make a correct diagnosis. Once the correct diagnosis has been made, the most effective treatment will suggest itself almost automatically.

chapter **ten**

how to answer
objections

Be Sure You Have a Prospect

I t would be futile to address the problem of answering objections until you know how to recognize a prospect with whom you can do business. Many general agents and trainers of bygone days summed up the job of prospecting in this manner: "Go out and kick the brush. If you flush out a person who has a *need*, who can *pay*, and who can *pass*, you've got a prospect!"

Every experienced life insurance underwriter, however, can cite dozens of cases where individuals who more than meet these qualifications still stubbornly resist all efforts to get them to provide adequate protection for their dependents. Why? For the simple reason that in many instances, the price-less ingredient of character was lacking. Before someone qualifies as a real prospect, he or she must have ambition and a sense of responsibility. The person must be gladly willing to make sacrifices for loved ones. Because the purchase of life insurance requires character, the sale of life insurance is a character sale. If you look closely and think about it carefully, you can recognize this cause-and-effect relationship in any "sales" situation.

Experienced life insurance salespeople have long recognized that many individuals offer little or no buyer resistance to most forms of property insurance. They will, however, persistently hold out against both logical and emotional appeals to cover the urgent and grave needs for family protection. Such people do not stop to realize that the devastating suffering—mental, emotional, and economic—imposed on unprepared spouses and children by the death of an under-insured individual exceeds anything they could possibly experience due to a property loss. True, a heavy property loss may cause a serious disturbance in an individual's affairs, but rarely does it change the entire future and destiny of several other human beings as does the death of the person who is responsible economically for his or her family.

Paradoxically, these individuals, during *their* lifetime, usually are good providers. They willingly provide for the necessities of life for their dependents, but seem unwilling to provide them with the necessities of life in the event of their own untimely death. That is why life insurance underwriters are called on for a higher order of skill and expertise in their work.

Purchasing life insurance involves character, so the sale of life insurance is a character sale. If you remember this, you will never catch yourself struggling to answer statements such as:

> "I don't want to leave a lot of money for my widow's or widower's new spouse to spend."

> "I want to enjoy my money."

> "My wife could go to work. She got along OK before we were married."

> "I intend to get some fun out of life."

If the prospect offers this kind of objection, you haven't got a prospect—not a real one. Do not even dignify such character-exposing statements by calling them objections. Recognize that no matter how expert your skills may be, you cannot sell everyone. The world-famous surgeon does not save every patient; the most devout and consecrated man of God does not convert every unbeliever; and the life member of the Million Dollar Round Table not only fails to close many sales, but often inadvertently sets up a competitor to take the sale.

Do not be a die-hard when you find that you have a prospect on your hands who does not possess the basic character necessary to buy what you are selling. If, in response to your desire to serve, the prospect persistently counters with absurd, inconsistent, weak, and flimsy objections or excuses, it is infinitely better to terminate the interview as quickly and as pleasantly as possible and continue on your way. To do otherwise is a costly waste of your time and energy. Remember, *whatever* business you are in, you are not in the reform business. Now and then it may cost a small sale or step toward your particular goal, but you will accomplish more in the long run when you know how to identify and approach intelligent, reasonable prospects.

> **Prospecting is like shaving.**
> **If you don't do it everyday,**
> **you look like a bum.**

Ladder of Acquaintanceship

It is an accepted fact that if the salesperson is a complete stranger to the prospect, the chance of making the sale is less than if they had some sort of relationship. Any kind of social connection makes a tremendous difference. That means that to develop your market, you first have to contact prospects in non-sales situations *before* approaching them directly about a sale.

One of the largest sales I ever made was through the contact of a man who was active in Sacramento-area social circles and who had met me through my performances in magic. Only after developing a non-sales relationship with him did I talk to him about working on an entertainment project together. Because a relationship was already in place, the sale was made *and* made with much less effort than if I had "cold called" him about this project. Imagine your prospect on various rungs of a ladder. The success rate jumps with each step up the ladder, as your relationship to the prospect becomes closer.

Ladder of Acquaintanceship

1st Rung: Complete stranger

2nd Rung: Someone you have heard of, but have never met

3rd Rung: Friend of an acquaintance

4th Rung: Relative or in-law of the prospect

5th Rung: Referral from a client, business partner, or friend

"You're a good editor with a promising future in the business. Why would you want to throw it all away to try to be a writer? I read your book. Frankly, it's not really that good."

This was a New York publisher's comments to James Michener about his first book, *Tales of the South Pacific*, for which Michener won a Pulitzer Prize.

chapter eleven

three kinds of
objections

O bjections usually fall into one of three categories. Here is how you can recognize and be ready to respond to each one.

Objections to the Salesperson

If the salesperson's appearance or manner is in any way objectionable to the prospect, it can terminate the interview before it even begins. In this case, the objection is not to the product or service being presented, but to the salesperson.

Some years ago, General Motors mailed 7 million questionnaires to and conducted 63,000 interviews with customers to find out how they reacted to various salespeople. The company compiled its results into the four-point guideline below:

• **Protect the prospect's ego**

Above everything else, the salesperson must safe guard the self-esteem of the prospect, because the desire to feel one's own importance is the deepest urge of human nature. Make prospects feel important. Make them feel that you are sincerely interested in their point of view.

• **Avoid overstatement**

There is something about the human brain that reacts unfavorably to extravagant claims and promises. Business professionals particularly are suspicious of salespeople whose statements are too strong or too impassioned. Enthusiasm is a good thing, but it is more effective when restrained and expressed in the form of deep earnestness.

• **Humor is effective, but must be used carefully**

Humor always helps get a new idea into a prospect's mind, but the attempt to use humor is dangerous unless you keep certain principles in mind. You can use the following tactics as "safe humor":

  · A joke on oneself or on the proposition being advocated

  · Something that is funny but directly or indirectly compliments the listener

  · A joke on an imaginary person or someone not intimately associated with the listener

• Always "save face" for the prospect

Saving face, or helping protect the prospect's honor and self-esteem, is one of the most important considerations in professional selling. Most individuals are willing to change their minds if the salesperson can help them justify their shift in position. Nobody wants to seem indecisive. Hence, your point of view should be presented in a way that is not directly contradictory to the prospect's existing viewpoint. Try to create a natural bridge from what they currently think to what you would like them to think.

Recognize Personal Ego

The first point above, "Protect the prospect's ego," is by no means a recent discovery. Many years ago, the great psychologist William James said, "The deepest principle of human nature is the desire to be appreciated." This ego, or feeling of personal worth, can be acknowledged in various ways:

• Reveal your knowledge of the prospect
Familiarize yourself with the prospect's name, birthday, children, golf scores, triumphs in business, hobbies, etc.

• Extol the individual's occupation
This is why clever politicians praise the farmer as "the backbone of the nation," the banker as "the pillar of society," the minister as "the saving grace," and to women voters they say, "The hand that rocks the cradle is the hand that rules the world."

• **Ask for favors**
Do this by asking for advice, the loan of a book or some other resource, etc. Do not, however, ask the prospect to expend undue time or energy on your behalf.

• **Ask an opinion**
Normally you should restrict your query to subjects on which you are not as knowledgeable as the prospect.

• **Imply that the prospect is superior to others in some way**
You can make comments such as, "This policy is available only to men in preferred occupations," or "We offer our service only to those who have or can purchase $100,000 of insurance or more."

• **Assume that the other person is in good financial condition**
You can make comments like, "Of course, your family is accustomed to every luxury now," or "Of course, you plan to send your children to college."

• **Be willing to serve the prospect**

This is a compliment to the prospect. In the quest for attaining your own goals, it makes sense to also look after the needs of others, especially the prospect. Genuinely attentive, caring service will quickly gain the prospect's confidence and trust in you.

• **Act with deference toward the prospect**

Nothing is more complimentary to a person than respectful yielding to his or her judgment. Always take every opportunity to genuinely say and do those things that make people feel bigger, better, more important.

The following books are highly useful resources in helping you understand and respond to a prospect's objections:

How to Win Friends and Influence People, by Dale Carnegie
The Technique of Handling People, by Donald A. Laird
The Psychology of Dealing With People, by Wendell White

Objections to Granting an Interview

Although usually listed as objections, the following are simply attempted brush-offs to avoid even a *discussion* about insurance. They are not real objections, but merely protests against interruptions or disturbances. They include:

"I am too busy."

"My wife has money."

"My situation is different."

"I don't need any more insurance."

"I'm worth more dead than alive."

"I have a friend in the business."

"I am not interested."

"See me after the first of the year."

The number and significance of these brush-offs are determined largely by the following factors:

• The origin or source of the lead

On average, a prospect that you cold call uses a stronger defense mechanism than someone whose friend or relative suggested that you call. Here are the five principal sources of leads, listed in descending order of resistance to an interview:

· Cold call

· Letters of introduction, or a referred lead

· Orphan policyholders

· Membership in the same lodge or club, neighbors

· Personal friends, relatives, the agent's own policyholders

Only very rarely do people in the last two groups offer any resistance at all to an interview if it is requested at a reasonably convenient time.

• Time and place not suitable for the interview

There is, as every successful salesperson knows, a right time and a right place for every sales interview. There is always a natural chemistry at work that can either launch or derail any interview. Be sensitive to the nonverbal communication involved.

• The prospect is not receptive

Your prospect my not be receptive because of other circumstances, such as an off day caused by domestic, financial, or business worries.

- **Prospect's attitude toward insurance or salespeople**

In this case, you may have to use the ideas from the four-point guideline under "Objections to the salesperson" to get the interview in the first place.

Such prospects may also feel unable to defend further objections once they do get into a conversation with the salesperson.

Experience proves that if the salesperson takes any or all of the above so-called objections literally or seriously, disappointment and failure will surely follow. Rather than recognize these attempted brush-offs as objections, experienced agents prefer to sympathize with the prospect and, in turn, continue with a sincere, no-strings-attached offer to approach the prospect at a more convenient time and place.

Countless attempts by prospects to get rid of the agent for any of the reasons above have been converted into sales that were pleasing to both the prospect and the agent, simply by the strategy of offering to do something in the way of service *for* the prospect.

For example, the salesperson could offer to:

· Calculate the prospect's Social Security benefits
· Service the prospect's present insurance plan

· Give advice and suggestions regarding wills, household budgets, etc.

The agent who hopes to succeed should become an expert in these matters.

The following is a sample script for how a successful salesperson can arrange a sales interview:

"Mr./Ms. Prospect, I have no reason to believe that you personally would be interested in a very popular plan of insurance that my company features, but the plan has helped solve the financial worries of many people in positions similar to yours. I would like to show it to you with the understanding that it will take me about ten minutes and that, if at the end of that time you are not sufficiently interested to discuss it further, I will leave immediately, remove your name from my prospect list, and not call on you again unless you invite me to do so. And, Mr./Ms. Prospect, I mean that. You see, I try to do business with men and women I feel are intelligent enough to make their own decisions in such matters, so you needn't hesitate in consenting to hear about our plan."

**It doesn't matter what you want;
it is what the customer wants.**

Objections to Closing the Deal

Here we have the critical moment in every interview. When selling life insurance, closing the deal means getting the prospect to sign the application. Let us assume that the prospect and the spouse have given their undivided attention to your presentation. Questions have been asked and answers given. The way seems clear for a quick and easy close. The application blank is unfolded with practiced casualness and then—you know the story only too well—the prospect tosses in an unexpected bombshell. Unless you are in control of the situation, the sale may be wrecked.

Is there a better or newer way to answer the honest objections? Is there a different way that will enable you to improve your ratio of sales interviews to closing interviews? In short, is there something you can do to simplify the problem of answering objections?

The Solution

The answer is an unqualified "yes"! The problem can be greatly simplified by:

- Fixing the problem in a way that will prevent many objections from being voiced in the first place.

- Realizing that it is ineffective and unnecessary to memorize answers to possible objections

- Knowing that every honest objection can be traced to root causes that, when fully under stood, will help you address the objection.

Preventing most objections

Most honest objections are not brought up while you are presenting the actual plan or program of insurance. They appear whenever you attempt to close. The number and importance of such objections are determined largely by your skill in fixing the problem. If you do an effective job of fixing the problem, it often happens that no objections are raised, giving you a green light for the close. In most cases, objections that do come up are usually not serious ones and can be easily prevented.

Let's look at the selling methods of agents A and B. Agent A is an insurance salesperson. Period. His sales presentation is filled with discussions of cash values, net costs, non-forfeiture provisions, settlement options, and ledger statements. He talks about what he has to offer, not what the prospect wants to hear. For that reason, he is one of the best-informed men in his agency, but he is weak at answering objections. His ratio of sales interviews to closing interviews is very unsatisfactory, and he often finds himself in an argument with the prospect about life insurance or about the prospect's attitude toward life insurance.

Agent B, on the other hand, is a student of the economic and social problems of life and living. He refuses to recognize objections to life insurance unless they are allowed to come up after he has fixed and discussed the greatest problem of life—the maintenance of income. Agent B talks about life, not death. He repeatedly reinforces that the prime reason for buying life insurance is not because people die, but rather because they, or their loved ones, must go on living.

Agent B knows that the prospect may honestly believe that he or she does not need more life insurance. But upon careful analysis, nine out of ten times additional needs are revealed. So Agent B acknowledges and fixes the problem, and further objections don't even arise.

The mere uncovering of a need, however, will not automatically cause a prospect to buy additional life insurance. Agent B knows that it is only when the prospect *feels* the need will he or she act on it. When a person feels a need for something, this feeling develops into a *want*, which compels whatever action is necessary to satisfy the need.

It is actually to your advantage when the problem is clear in the prospect's mind. It is then much easier to answer any objections. You simply emphasize the problem and the urgency of solving it instead of entering into an argument about the specific objection itself.

Agent B knows that he is selling a service, and that only way to make the prospect feel an urgent need for this service is through the right kind of persuasion. He knows that the facts of life cannot be changed: The prospect needs or wants more capital, income-producing property, or life insurance to carry out future plans. So why should Agent B hesitate to discuss these things? In other words, he assumes that the prospect is seeking the truth.

Agent B agrees wholeheartedly that two conditions are always required to close the deal:

The prospect must honestly recognize the need

and the uniqueness of life insurance as the best and only solution to that need.

The prospect must have a compelling desire to provide that solution to his or her family.

Lastly, agent B never forgets that if the life insurance underwriter tries to "sell insurance" he will have to sell it. But if he will stop trying to sell insurance and make it his business to "fix problems," the person for whom he fixes the problem will ask him about insurance.

Answering Objections

Now that you understand objections, how will you respond to them? Do you usually experience a momentary blackout or uneasiness when reaching for an answer—an answer you may have read or heard, one that you try to recall, one that you thought you had *memorized* (or wish that you had)? Do you, at the same time, find that you are completely relaxed in your discussions with skeptical prospects over questions concerning the relative merits of term and cash value plans, monthly income and lump-sum settlements, Social Security provisions, beneficiary arrangements, etc.?

If your answer to these questions is "yes," we must conclude that you are confident in your knowledge of life insurance but that you lack confidence when it comes to selling. Knowledgeable and skilled salespeople fearlessly discuss or explain the provisions of the contract, various policy forms, rate construction, insurance principles, etc., without ever having memorized a single line of print. No one puts words in their mouths, and no two explanations or answers are ever exactly the same. These salespeople simply draw on a ready reserve of information. Likewise, a satisfying response to an *honest* objection should be as spontaneous and effortless, simply because you know your subject so well.

> **"You can't play the piano, and God knows you can't sing. You'd better learn how to weave chairs so you can support yourself."**
>
> **This was a comment from one of Ray Charles' teachers.**

While I have not provided ways to respond to all the specific objections *you* will face, I have provided a very workable model for doing so. Remember that objections are the symptoms you need to make a correct diagnosis of the prospect's real cause of resistance. Remember, too, that if you can identify this root cause of an objection, you will find a way to answer it based on your knowledge and passion to succeed.

I have given you stockpile of secrets, suggestions, and strategies to which you can add your own thoughts, ideas, and experiences. I suggest that you organize and arrange all this material carefully. Study it. But do not memorize it! You will enjoy an effortless and spontaneous means of handling objections on your way to accomplishing any goal.

part four

introduction

Part Four of this book includes remarkable stories about individuals who have successfully used *The Fine Art of Persuasion* in their personal and professional lives. Through this art of "selling," they have first convinced themselves to pursue their goals and dreams, and then used the insights, techniques, and strategies from this book to gain the support of others. These stories show how the power of persuasion—"selling" to yourself and others—can help you accomplish heights you may never have dreamed possible or to overcome what might seem like impossible obstacles. I hope these stories will inspire you to raise your sights and achieve greatness in *your* life.

chapter twelve

success stories

Arthur's Stories:

Arthur Banchero is a businessman and a friend whom I have known for many years. He shared these next two stories with me as inspiration for self-improvement:

Persuade Yourself to Try Something New

A number of years ago the Puget Sound Light and Power Company developed a new iron for ironing clothes. There was one particular salesman in the sales department who wasn't particularly good-looking and he didn't dress that well, but month after month he sold more irons than anybody else. Over time, the other salespeople would ask him, "What is it? What magic words, what powers of persuasion are you using that enable you to outsell everybody else?" The salesman simply replied, "I don't really say anything." He would never divulge his secret because he didn't feel he had a secret.

At the end of his career, when this top salesman had been with the company for twenty-five years, the sales manager said, "You have been our top salesman all these years. You are retiring and leaving now. So please, tell me what your secret is." The salesman said, "Well, you know that when I first joined your sales force, you set me up as the partner of another salesperson. We went to the first house and asked if we could demonstrate our iron. The woman agreed, so we went into the house. She made us a cup of coffee and we did our demonstration. She was interested, but she said she had to talk to her husband about it. In other words, our powers of persuasion were not strong enough at that point.

"We went to the next house and the same thing happened. That went on at house after house. I noticed that at the end of the day we had only made about nine or ten calls, and we had only sold about three irons. The next day, we had to go back out and repeat the process all over again. Our success rate seemed very low for all the effort we were putting out, demonstrating the iron at each house.

"When I started making calls on my own, I tried a different approach. I would go up to the front door and say, 'Madam, I have an iron here that is the best on the market. It will save you a lot of work. Are you interested?' If she said no, I would simply thank her and go on to the next house, then the next, and the next, and the next. I was making about thirty to forty calls a day when the rest of your salespeople were making about seven or eight calls a day. I found out that the more calls I made the more successful I was at selling. So you see, I am not much to look at and I don't have a good voice, but I had the law of averages on my side."

This is an excellent example of how to combine the power of persuasion with good judgment and planning. To persuade doesn't mean to push; it means to prepare a path. You can persuade others, but sometimes the most important person to persuade is yourself. And in this case, it was the salesman persuading himself, as much as anybody else, to try a new approach. And it worked!

Persuade yourself to turn time into profit

The second story is about Arthur Banchero himself. He told me this story about a meeting he had with Thomas Mellon, the sales manager of Westics Electric Heater Company. One day, while talking to his sales department, Mr. Mellon asked his salespeople this question: "Have you ever figured out what it takes to pay your salary?" (In those days it was about $23,000 a year.) "We also provide an office for you, which is another $7,000 or $8,000 a year, and car expenses, which total another $8,000 a year. All together, it costs us about $160 a day to keep you on the road.

"Now let's analyze one of your typical days. You get up to go to the office. You go meet some of your friends down the hall. You talk a little and then you have a cup of coffee. You make a couple of phone calls, maybe to your friends, maybe to a prospective customer. Finally, you get out of the office about 9:00 or 9:30. You head for the first prospect. (Today we make appointments. In those days, it was all cold calling.) You get to the prospect's office and talk to the receptionist for a while if the prospect is busy. Finally, after about fifteen minutes you get in to see the prospect. If you already knew him, you ask how the fishing is, or did he watch the football games over the weekend, and how is the family, etc.

"So you are in the office about half an hour to an hour before you even start talking about the product. Finally you get to the product and just as you start talking about it, the prospect gets a phone call. Finally, when the phone call is over, you finish talking about the product. After about fifteen or twenty minutes, you leave. Then you take another hour and forty minutes to repeat the same routine at the next call.

"Now," said Mr. Mellon, "I want you to figure out how many hours you talk to the prospect about the product on a typical day like this. Subtract the time you spend sharing fishing stories and the time you spend talking to the receptionist. If you are lucky, you spoke about the product for an hour and a half, total, all day. If it costs us $160 dollars a day to keep you on the road, then those two or three calls you made cost us about $50 to $60 a call. At that cost, how should you be using your time? What should you tell a prospect? How should you practice persuasion? You had better know what you are talking about, and you had better be able to present the highlights quickly and effectively. You are on stage such a short time—you'd better have a good presentation. Be prepared."

The point here is that again, by using the power of persuasion on yourself, you would overcome your obstacles—which in this case were the receptionist and conversations about football and fishing. In doing so, you would probably get to the source of the sale a lot more quickly. In turn, by stripping the sale down to its essential elements and by skillfully motivating yourself and the prospect, you would probably increase your number of sales substantially.

Mike's and Linda's Stories:

The next two stories are from Linda and Mike Abrams, whom I met many years ago. Linda has since become my associate on a number of projects. Mike and Linda married shortly after I met them. Mike is a successful businessman and real estate developer. I think you will appreciate the hurdles he had to overcome. It took a lot of personal persuasion and motivation. Linda tells her story first:

Have Faith in Your Dreams

"When I was fourteen years old, my parents took me to hear a motivational speaker who was appearing in our hometown. I was totally captivated by the message he delivered regarding how I could achieve whatever I wanted in life if I clearly set my goals, worked hard, and had faith that I could achieve it. This speaker taught the importance of making a plan book and writing down your goals, starting five years out and working backward to one-year and daily plans. At age fourteen, I started to work on my plan book. I got a binder and started cutting out pictures of places I wanted to go and accomplishments I wanted to achieve.

"One of the goals I wrote down was traveling. I cut out a lot of pictures to go with it. But my family was of very moderate means, and one thing we rarely did was any type of traveling. I dreamed of traveling to Europe or Asia and especially of taking a trip on a cruise ship. Thirty years ago, only the very wealthy could ever consider spending the amount of money required to take one of those luxurious trips. I had a burning desire for this to happen. It was an important part of my plan book, but I did not know how it would ever manifest itself.

"Years went by. I continued to study and practice my talent and enjoyed a lot of success with what I did. But the thought of that trip stayed with me, year after year.

"One day, when I was twenty-one years old, I was standing at the kitchen sink doing the dishes. I was thinking how bored I was, that not very much was going on, and that maybe I needed a new direction. My goals now seemed fuzzy and unobtainable. I was discouraged and felt like tearing up my plan book and throwing it away.

"At that precise moment, the telephone rang, and there was an unfamiliar voice on the other end. This man gave me his name, although it meant nothing to me. I had never heard of him. He began telling me that he was a magician and was looking for a partner to travel to parts of Asia and perform magic with him. At first I thought maybe he was a quack. I said, 'Who are you, and how did you get my name and telephone number?' Furthermore, I had never performed any magic.

"The man then told me the person's name who had recommended me to him, and this gave me some level of comfort. He asked if he could come over and show me what this was all about. I said yes, and wouldn't you know, he was at my door in five minutes. He was the motivated type. He spread out before me a brochure on the most luxurious, expensive cruise that traveled throughout Asia. This cruise cost paying passengers $30,000 each. Here, right before my eyes, was the cruise, the trip of my dreams, that I had put in my plan book at age fourteen. I was astounded. Now it was here before me, all for free, if I could learn some simple magic tricks. I did have the stage experience necessary.

"But it got even better. The man invited me to his home that evening to look at videotapes of his magic act and to meet his family. When I arrived at his home, I realized I had been there before, at a party. I couldn't believe it. This man was Bob Brown. He had taken the same motivational course I had years earlier and had thrown a party at his home afterward for the very speaker who had taught me to make my plan book.

"Somehow, when we set our dreams and goals down on paper, the universe seems to help bring it to pass, even for a fourteen-year-old. Just be prepared for the opportunity to come. I didn't know it was coming, but I was prepared. Luck is when opportunity meets with preparation. Be sure to systematically set your goals and dreams down in writing. Attend to those goals. Again, see figure 2, You and Your Dreams.

"I continued to apply myself to goal-setting, planning, and believing in a higher power to help direct my course. I continued to work in magic, improving my skills and performance. Not long after this first encounter with Bob, an opportunity came up for us to perform in Monte Carlo. I told Bob that if we were going to Monte Carlo, we should perform for Princess Grace of Monaco and Prince Rainier. He said he would talk to his contacts and see if there was any possibility that this could happen. Princess Grace had been my idol as a child, and I wanted in the worst way to perform for her.

"This trip was my big opportunity, and this presentation was my primary purpose for going. As time went on, however, it seemed that the chance for this opportunity to become a reality was fading. There only seemed to be obstacles in the way and the final answer was no. I continued to believe that somehow things would work out. We left on the trip with no possibility in sight. But I just knew that somehow, some way, I would not leave Monte Carlo before I had an opportunity to perform for Princess Grace.

"After we performed at a local hotel in Monte Carlo for a few days, Bob and I were contacted by Dieter Friedrich, the regional manager of the TWA office handling all the reservations and activities on the French Rivera, including many of the traveling activities for Princess Grace. Bob had been advised to contact Dieter with the intention of being introduced to some potential clients. Dieter informed us that there was going to be a private party for the royal family and close friends. They needed some entertainment for the evening, and would we be interested in performing for them? Of course we would. And we did!

"Once again, the power of belief and personal persuasion to keep on keeping on brought forth the desired goal. All through life I have continued to have faith and belief that my dreams would become reality and that obstacles are only stepping-stones to success.

Sell yourself rich.

"After five years of being the featured performer at San Francisco Forty Niner's football games, winning numerous beauty and talent competitions, and performing extensively on cruise ships throughout Europe, South America, Asia, and the Middle East, I entered the business world.

"I began my career as the manager of the Rio Del Oro Tennis Club. I moved from there into the commercial real estate development business. It was 1978, and women who worked in commercial real estate were rare. After working in the business for six years, with $5,000 in the bank, I struck out on my own and began successfully developing and remodeling commercial retail centers. During this time I

113

founded Commercial Real Estate Women (CREW) in Orange County, California, a national organization that brings together women in the commercial real estate industry to network, promote business, and support one another. During this time, I met and married my husband Mike Abrams, a very successful commercial real estate developer. I later teamed up with him in developing commercial and residential properties in Southern California."

Fry One Egg at a Time

Mike Abrams is a very successful real estate developer, having amassed a multimillion-dollar financial statement by his early thirties. He and his wife, Linda, thought that they were set for life. Little did they realize that the worst recession since the 1930s was about to hit California. It was the early 1990s. Linda tells the following story:

"It seemed like all we had worked for had not only vanished before our eyes, but it also became a nightmare we could never have imagined. Not only had we lost all of our money, but every property we owned also became a huge liability. We now had not a multimillion-dollar financial statement, but a negative multimillion-dollar financial statement. Banks, investors, and vendors all wanted to be paid immediately. What should we do? Was bankruptcy the right answer? All of our advisors said it was the only way we could survive. We were, for all intents and purposes, bankrupt, but decided that declaring bankruptcy was not for us. We would solve our problems.

"We had 100 investors knocking on our door. We also needed to work out close to a million dollars of debt on our properties with many different banks. We had two young children and elderly parents who needed our financial support. We had no cash. We no longer owned a house. We had obligations of $150,000 per month, with only $200,000 left in the bank. We were in a protracted recession with no new business looming on the horizon. It felt like we were falling, falling, falling, and had no idea where the bottom was. We were both depressed. How would we survive?

"I asked my husband how we would handle all the problems that all loomed simultaneously. He thought for a moment and then recounted his experience working as a short-order cook in a restaurant in his early twenties. At breakfast, the restaurant was unbelievably busy. He looked at all the orders for eggs and became overwhelmed wondering how he would ever get all those orders of eggs to the customers. His boss looked at him and said, 'Fry one egg at a time and keep going. Before you know it, they will all be done.' So he focused only on the one order of eggs in front of him, not all the orders piled around him. Sure enough, it worked. Mike said that we should do same thing: Fry one egg at a time.

"That simple philosophy worked, and now, twelve years later, every egg has been fried. Mike and I survived the nightmare. He rebuilt his real estate business to be even more successful than before. When starting to apply for business loans once again, lenders heard his story, and even though he had no personal money, they began giving him loans on new building projects. They said, 'You're just the kind of borrower we want to do business with.' "

Lauri's Story:
You Can't Reach the Stars Alone

This story shows the real power of persuasion when a person uses it in their early years as a force to keep on keeping on toward long-term goals. Today, Lauri Thompson is an entertainment attorney with the Las Vegas law firm Quirk & Tratos. She is the president of the American Association of University Women, Las Vegas Branch, and on the board for Variety Children's Charity. Lauri is married to Allen Bracken, production stage manager for the world-famous magician, Lance Burton. Lauri and Allen have two sons, Nikolas and Alexander.

Lauri looks back on her early years, when she was eight or nine years old, as the point when her career started. This was when she first started trying to persuade herself to create and follow her life goals. Lauri's story exemplifies the rich rewards you can achieve when persuasion is used to its greatest advantage:

"Dreams are something we do alone, but goals are only accomplished with the help of others. I suppose we all have a different way of accomplishing our goals; mine has always been first to look at whether the goal is a possibility. If it is a possibility, can I make it a probability? If it is a probability, can I make it likely to happen? I then gather all the information and assets I have at my disposal, including the ability to depend on others. Of course, the ability to depend on others is directly related to your ability to persuade them to help you accomplish your goals. We need to not only to persuade ourselves that something is likely to happen, but we need to persuade others that it is a noble cause, worthy of their time and resources.

"I decided when I was eight or nine years old that I wanted to go to law school, for some noble reasons and for some very selfish reasons. Selfishly, I was scared to death that I would get into an occupation that would have a ceiling—that I would accomplish everything there was to accomplish and still have life left to live, with no purpose. I realized that the law was always evolving. You could learn and grow forever, with only the sky as the limit. For more noble reasons, I saw 'collective potential' as being one of most important goals toward which to strive. Each of us has the opportunity to accomplish more with the help of others. The law helps us to work and live together and, more specifically, it provides a framework for predictability. We are all more willing to put forth efforts when we can rely on others.

"I did not go to law school right after college, however. I was a performer for twenty years before the opportunity presented itself for me to go to law school. I had worked as a classical ballet dancer, a live stage performer in musical theater, a television actress, a spokesperson for major corporations, and a print model. During the twenty years of performing in all of these capacities, I kept my eyes and ears open in order to try and understand the basic structure of the business side of the industry. I learned how collective talents were incorporated into the development of an entertainment project.

"I became fascinated with the concept of persuading people to work toward a common goal. I began to produce shows, beginning with shows in which I performed and eventually producing shows in which I did not perform. I realized how valuable the person is who can identify people and their individual talent and bring them together to accomplish a goal. I began to see that a law degree would take me one step closer to my goals.

"I had been waiting for a law school to open in Las Vegas where I was performing in the Follies Bergere. The law school was delayed, so I finally decided to look for a way to attend another law school. I first started investigating to see if it was possible; and if it were possible, could I make it probable; and if it were probable, could I make it a reality?

"It took a lot of personal persuading, but I finally convinced myself it would be possible for me to fly to San Diego to attend the University of San Diego Law School during the day and fly back to perform my two shows at night in Las Vegas. The next step was to persuade the people around me that they should offer their support and help facilitate this educational program. Of course, the first people I needed to persuade were those at U.S.D. I needed to make them believe that I would be an asset to their school and that I could take the valuable education they offer and use it successfully as an attorney after I graduated. I was very fortunate to be accepted as one of the entering law students for the class of 1998. I also needed to persuade my producer that this was possible and that it would not have a detrimental effect on my performance in the show.

"During my first two years of law school, every day that I had classes I boarded a plane at 6:30 a.m., flew from Las Vegas to San Diego, attended classes all day, and then boarded a plane around 5:00 p.m. in order to get back to Las Vegas to be back on stage by 7:00 p.m. I studied between my numbers in the show, between the shows themselves, and on the plane traveling both ways. The curtain came down on my second show around midnight. I would quickly hurry home, wash off my makeup, and catch a few hours of sleep before having to get up and start over again the next day.

"During the first two years of law school, I maintained this schedule. I then stopped performing in the Follies Bergere and began working at the law firm of Quirk & Tratos in Las Vegas to prepare myself to practice in the field of entertainment law. This position meant that I would not have to fly every day to San Diego; I would only have to fly three times a week.

"The practice of law proved to be quite a challenge. It took many hours of concentration and hard work to learn a new profession that would allow me to apply talents garnered from my previous career. Now, I meet daily with people in an effort to help them understand and meet their goals and objectives. I spend a great deal of time trying to persuade other talented people, on behalf of my clients, to help facilitate my clients' goals. I also spend a great deal of my time trying to persuade people that our differences can be resolved without the necessity of a court's ruling through litigation.

"Without the ability to persuade others, I don't believe that we can ever reach our own true potential. I truly believe that we are all here with the purpose of facilitating each other in accomplishing our mutual goals and dreams. I always like to quote from Sir Isaac Newton: 'If I have seen farther, it is from standing on the shoulders of giants.' Sometimes we are on top, reaching for the stars. At other times we are the giant, and others are standing on our shoulders to reach toward and grasp their own dreams."

Bob's Story:

This is one of my own earliest success stories. It appeared as an article, written by contributing editor Lassor A. Blumenthal, in The American Salesman magazine. The article shows how more than 3,505 employees and approximately 6,000 dependents enrolled in the insurance-benefit program I set up for their company. It took a lot of persuasion, then following through with the board of directors, department heads, and eventually with all the employees, to make the program a success. It is a dramatic illustration of the power of persuasion at work. It is also an exemplary example of the difference between "hard sell" and "heart sell."

Here's what happened:

"3,505 Buying Influences Decided This Sale"
by Lassor A. Blumenthal

One morning Robert F. Brown, an insurance sales-person in Sacramento, California, opened a letter in his morning mail and read:

Dear Mr. Brown:
Our company is interested in receiving a proposal from you relative to serving as a consultant in the development of an employee health and accident insurance program. This request is being sent to a number of individuals in California who have been recommended as having broad experience in the group health and accident insurance field.

So began a sale that ended seven months later in nearly half a million dollars' worth of business and eventually grew to $4 million. Furthermore, it employed an extraordinarily unorthodox persuading and selling technique. This is the story of how Bob did it.

"I knew I had three problems," Bob said recently. "First, I had to convince the board of directors that I was the man they should deal with. Next, I would have to persuade them to accept the program that I felt was best for them. Third, I'd have to persuade the employees to sign up in large numbers."

The letter, signed by the CEO, had asked Bob to outline the approach he would suggest and to submit references within two weeks.

Self-selling: Before answering, Bob did some research. He got a copy of the company's current employee insurance program. It was an outdated, minimal health-and-accident plan. A phone call to the accounting department office told him that the employees were required to pay all the premiums and file their own claims.

"When I replied," Bob said, "I didn't criticize their plan. I simply wanted to give them confidence in me."

His two-page response was a small masterpiece of quiet selling and persuasion. He began by thanking them, and in his second sentence said, "I am ready to go to work for you immediately."

Why the outspoken enthusiasm? Said Bob: "Clients appreciate the human touch. No matter how businesslike they are, they want to know that you, as an individual, are eager for their business."

He wrote that his approach would be to (a) take a statistical survey of the employees and discuss this data with interested specialists, such as the local medical society and local hospitals, in order to figure costs properly; (b) talk to local health and welfare administrators to find out how they kept premiums down; and (c) discuss the whole matter with the company's department heads, because "No plan is any better than an employee's understanding of it."

Bob was offering to do an enormous amount of work. "I wanted to show that I was willing to give; I wasn't interested solely in getting," he said.

Describing his background, Bob wrote, "Investigation will prove that we are *second to none* in installing programs." The reason for the sentence, Bob explained, was that "no matter what you're selling, if you can show you're an expert in some area, the prospect will have more confidence in you."

Although Bob mentioned that his clients included both public and private organizations, he gave no names. His reason: "I wanted to encourage them to call for more information."

First in first lap: The tactic worked. A couple of weeks later, Bob received a call from an analyst on the company staff who had been assigned to oversee the project. "He was polite, but not overly friendly," Bob recalled. "He said that he'd like names of my references. I gave him the names of groups similar to his. He told me I'd hear from him again and hung up."

"I was tempted to call the analyst," said Bob. The board had decided to appoint Bob "Broker of Record" to represent the company in buying and installing a plan. To this day, only the board members know precisely why they selected Bob. Undoubtedly, one reason is that Bob, who was forty-two years old, had been preparing for this sale for more than ten years.

"As early as 1951," he said recently, "I became convinced that mass marketing was the wave of the future. You could see it in supermarkets and discount stores. In insurance, it was the rise of group plans."

Bob foresaw a severely restricted future for himself unless he did something about it. He could see that in the insurance field—as in industry in general—the group specialist would be coming in to handle a problem, then flying off to troubleshoot in another part of the country. Bob felt, however, that no one-shot specialist could do as thorough a job as a local salesman who lived close to the customer.

"So I decided to become a local salesman who was also a specialist," he said. "I took university and home-study courses, read books, and joined organizations."

Gradually, Bob began selling larger and larger group plans. Now he had sold himself to the board for what would be the largest sale of his career thus far, and one of the largest sales ever handled by the insurance company he selected.

"The next phase was to sell the board on the best possible program," said Bob. This meant that he had to (a) decide what program was best, (b) find an insurance company that would supply the coverage, and (c) persuade the board to go along.

To select the best program, Bob first had to gather a mass of statistics on the employees: their age, sex, and income-distribution, the kinds of jobs they had, where they worked, etc. The analyst, his liaison, while cooperative, was understandably surprised at the blizzard of information that Bob requested. He pointed out the workload it would put on the already overburdened employees. And he wondered, did Bob really need all this information?

Bob's answer made sense to the analyst: "The more information we can give the insurance companies, the better they can tailor a plan to your specific needs. In the long run, it will save you money."

High hurdle: During this time, Bob learned about one of his major obstacles. The company analyst told him that the employer was planning to contribute approximately $3 a month per employee to the plan. Bob knew that a good plan would cost between $5 and $6 per person and that no group plan would win wide employee acceptance unless the employer paid for it all. Consequently, he was going to have to persuade the board to pay all costs and to double its planned contribution.

Encounter that counted: Bob first met with the board on November 6. The five members sat on a dais at one end of a large, rectangular hall. In front of them was a lectern, from which Bob spoke.

The analyst introduced Bob, who thanked the board for selecting him then gave the members a memorandum spelling out his duties. "This suggested the terms they might offer in a letter to me," he recalled. "When you are working with corporate officers, you should have your relationship clearly defined. Otherwise, if a change brings in new officials, you might have to sell yourself all over again. I decided to get off to an easy start with this routine matter."

Then Bob began his forty-five-minute presentation. It was remarkable for two reasons. First, he supported every point—almost every sentence—with a document. Second, in defiance of an all-but-universal sales rule, he did not use one document from his own field—the insurance industry.

Bob opened a folder marked "Why You Need Insurance," inside of which was a thick pile of newspaper and magazine articles on the rising costs of medical care.

The trick of selling

Although he's a proficient magician, Bob Brown does not incorporate magic in his presentations. He does, however, occasionally show a client a bit of magic to relax him. Once, after selling one prospect a very large policy with a premium of $750 a year, Bob showed the man how to do a baffling card trick. "That," said the client wryly, "is undoubtedly the most expensive trick that I have learned."

"Gentlemen," he said, "if you were to spend several months researching, you would finally assemble the material collected in this folder. My showing it to you now will save you that time."

The Trick of Selling

Although he's a proficient magician, Bob Brown does not incorporate magic in his presentations. He does, however, occasionally show a client a bit of magic to relax him or her. Once, after selling one prospect a very large policy with a premium of $750 a year, Bob showed the man how to do a baffling card trick. "That," said the client wryly, "is undoubtedly the most expensive trick that I have learned."

Having secured their interest by suggesting that he would explain a complex subject in minutes instead of months, Bob continued his courtroom technique, holding up a startling news headline: "PARENTS FORCED TO SELL HOME TO PAY DAUGHTER'S HOSPITAL BILLS."

He walked to the dais, letting each board member get a close look at the exhibit, then returned to his platform and explained that medical costs had been skyrocketing largely because of expensive new drugs and "miracle" surgery.

He documented each point, sometimes reading from a medical journal, sometimes from a magazine or newspaper. Not once did he talk about insurance. After about twelve minutes, he summarized, saying: "Now that you know the needs of the company employees, we can turn to the next question: How do we supply those needs?"

As Bob recalls: "I assumed that while they wanted insurance, they didn't fully know why. There is no point in trying to close a sale if a person does not think he or she needs your product. I wanted to be sure that they fully understood the need for the product I was going to recommend."

Standing on principles: Bob opened his next folder, titled "Design Concepts," which contained another hefty file of clippings. He was now going to tell the board about certain principles that should govern an insurance program.

If the board agreed to the principles, Bob felt that they would want the specific policies, which embodied these principles, even if, as Bob knew, they would cost more than the anticipated $3.

These materials were also from third-party sources. He read from a business magazine article explaining that high hospital bills were largely the result of a lack of control over insurance payments. From a second magazine he cited figures showing that the greater a person's insurance coverage, the longer that person was likely to stay in the hospital. Consequently, the insurance company's payments were higher, which led directly to higher premiums. The only way to keep premiums low was to insist on certain controls.

Bob knew that an un-instructed board might have decided to buy a more liberal policy with a total premium of, say $13 a month per employee. Nevertheless, the company would have stuck to the $3 contribution, and let the employees contribute the balance.

This would demolish his goal of having the company pay all the basic costs and therefore achieving a high proportion of employees signing up. Only with a high rate of participation, could he get an insurance company to quote a low price. The key to this intricate chain lay in the board's acceptance of four basic principles, which, in effect, eliminated superfluous coverage.

Because they were the core of his argument, Bob had written out everything he was going to say about the principles. He distributed copies to all the members and then read the statement aloud.

To weight his argument, he named the well-known actuary who had devised the principles, and explained that the man had discussed them at conferences and before a U.S. Senate committee. The principles, in short, were clad in the armor of formal, prestigious references.

Pricing and policing: When he finished reading, Bob turned briefly to price. Without discussing the $3 figure, he showed that comparable coverage bought by other public groups, including the state employees of California, came closer to $6. "I didn't want to press it," said Bob, "I just wanted to make them aware of the going price for the best coverage."

> **1% Inspiration, 99% Perspiration**
> *To sell this group policy, Bob Brown estimates that he worked approximately sixteen hours on the sale before he was appointed "Broker of Record." He spent most of this time on research. After his appointment, he estimates that he spent about four months getting the plan installed and fully operative.*

Bob had one more folder, titled "Controls and Policing," also containing third-party clippings referring to specific causes that should go into a sound program. One practical proposal was that all claims be paid according to the value assigned in the California Medical Association's book Relative Value Studies. This would protect an insurance company against exorbitant doctors' fees and prevent employees from having to pay the difference between a high doctor's bill and the insurance allowance.

After his presentation, Bob asked for permission

to give the identical talk to department heads and representatives of the employees' union. He also suggested that the board send him further instructions on specific plans he should investigate.

On November 26, Bob received a letter from the board, suggesting that we work out three different plans for medical-hospital coverage. Two would be traditional group programs. The third would be based on the four principles.

Working with a number of insurance companies, Bob figured out costs for the three plans, as well as for additional optional policies covering disability income, life insurance, and employee dependents. With the help of an artist, he drew up a brochure describing the three plans. "From my work as a magician," Bob said recently, "I knew the value of color in enhancing a presentation. I used colors to illustrate the benefits of the three plans, and kept numbers at a minimum."

Back to the board: In Bob's second meeting with the board, he distributed a brochure to each member, and went over it page by page. Probably the most persuasive figures were the brief ones at the bottom of each page, describing costs. The two traditional plans would cost about $13 per person per month, the third one between $5 and $6.

Now, for the first time, Bob asked the board for a commitment to pay the entire cost of the program. He elaborated on a point that the analyst had made earlier: A plan that all employees accepted would be an excellent recruiting tool. Undoubtedly, the board also realized that a universally accepted plan would serve as a useful fringe benefit at the next union bargaining session.

Although the board refused to make a commitment, it agreed that Bob's third plan was clearly superior, and authorized him to get bids from insurance companies.

Bid for bids: Several carriers were not eager to quote. In the first place, the company work force included a large number of women employees and hospital employees, who historically have a high loss ratio. Second, the employees were scattered over a large geographical area, making their claims expensive to handle.

One underwriter told Bob, "We'd be interested in quoting on the disability income plan because we've had a lot of experience there. But we're reluctant to go into the medical coverage because you have so many dubious risks."

Bob used the carrot-and-stick principle. "I suspect that the company will select one carrier," he told the man. "If you want part of the business, you'll probably have to quote all of it. But remember, the board has agreed to strict controls; this will limit your losses. Also, this will probably be a very big account. There are 3,500 employees, and we expect most of them to sign up for optional as well as basic benefits.

In the end, virtually every company Bob approached submitted a bid, and he prepared for his third and final presentation. He drew up a spreadsheet that showed prices quoted by each of the carriers for the basic medical plan as well as for the optional extra benefits. On January 3 at 9:30 a.m.,

Bob walked into the boardroom. He noticed a number of independent brokers in the audience. At approximately 10:00, he was called upon to present his program.

Bob gave each board member a spreadsheet. Some of the supervisors were probably surprised that Bob had identified carriers only by letter.

"I felt that the company should be picked on the basis of what it offered," Bob said.

To forestall any anxiety about the carriers' reputations, Bob briefly discussed the background of each one by name, explaining that he had approached only top-quality firms.

After reviewing all minor variations from the specifications, the board selected the low bidder, which had quoted a price of $5.75.

Monkey wrench that missed: Then trouble broke out. The chairman asked if anyone in the audience wished to comment. A local broker with a large Sacramento firm reeled off a long list of impressive clients, and sought to belittle Bob by declaring, "This plan is simply no good." Two others in the audience also made their views known.

The chairman asked Bob: "Would you care to comment?"

Bob's response took less than two minutes. He said his critics had no basis for challenging his qualifications after his appointment by the company and that their criticisms of the plan resulted from their unfamiliarity with the material that had guided the board's decision. "This type of plan," he reminded listeners, "has been recommended by the National

Conference of Health and Welfare plans, composing the country's largest holders of group insurance. None of these gentlemen belongs to that conference."

Apparently, the brevity and dignity of Bob's response impressed the board; they adopted his idea of paying the entire premium.

"When the meeting adjourned at 11:30," Bob said, "the most vociferous of the critics walked up, held out his hand, and said, 'Congratulations. I figured I had nothing to lose by trying.'"

Mustering his troops: By the end of the day, Bob had written the losing carriers and called the insurance company chosen to do the job to ask for help in installing the program. Pressure was intense, because the program was to start in about a month. Hundreds of administrative details remained to be worked out, from setting up claim procedures to selecting the color of paper for the employees' application forms.

(The home office sent three men. They collaborated closely as a team, worked long hours, and in about a week the mechanics for the entire plan had been worked out.)

In the next two weeks, Bob executed the last phase of the sale: winning the employees' acceptance. This involved two steps: teaching the payroll clerks how to handle the procedures, and getting the employees to sign up in large numbers.

In talking to the clerks, Bob again relied heavily on visual techniques, using a huge enlargement of the color chart in the brochure he'd shown the supervisors.

In educating the employees, Bob had begun two weeks before by writing a column for the union newspaper and by sending all of the employees a preliminary announcement brochure with a cover letter signed by the CEO. He saw to it that no one was called in at the last minute to sign on the dotted line.

For the final closing, Bob assembled a small army headed by a team of four men from his home office; in addition, there were Bob, his brother Dick, and two other Sacramento insurance men. Bob had given each person a large blowup of a specially devised single-page application form—the crucial element—to use in their presentations.

"Speed was vital," Bob said recently. "If you stretch it out, the employees you've talked to start discussing it with those you haven't yet reached. Inevitably, the story gets garbled, and you have to do twice as much work."

Pretty package: The squad went to work on January 17 to thoroughly inform the employees. Four days later, they had finished, Out of more than 3,500 employees, 3,505 signed up for the basic plan, compared with 700 under the old plan. Those who signed up for the optional plans, at their own expense, increased proportionately, thus swelling the total premiums paid to approximately $450,000 a year.

"There was no magic in it," Bob remarked. "It was simply a matter of educating the prospects to buy the better product through the use of professional persuasion."

With blessings,
Bob Brown

Get all that you want.
Give all that you can.

About the Author

Born in Sacramento, California only 82 years ago, leading guru Bob Brown's career has humble beginnings, selling magazines door-to-door when he was eight years old. He graduated from Sacramento City College, served his country overseas, and began working for Mutual of New York back in 1948. Not a born salesman, as it might seem, Bob studied hard and succeeded in his quest to become one of the company's "Top 50" sales professionals. In his 52 years with MONY, he topped that list once. He qualified for MONY's promotion in TIME magazine for leading producers.He was frequently among the very elite "Top 25" in the entire company. Acknowledged as a master of the sales process and one of the most successful sales professionals in the business, his talks are filled with tales and techniques from an amazing career that includes the record of 46 consecutive years as a very distinguished member of the Million Dollar Round Table, with lifetime sales exceeding a half-billion dollars.

A self-made millionaire, Bob insists he is just getting warmed up. As a respected presenter, Bob travels the world to speak at conventions and business meetings with such topics as "Sales Secrets from Sixty Years of Success" and "The Fine Art of Persuasion". His speeches are inspirational and entertaining, filled with humor and practical, time-tested advice.

Bob is active in community service, having been awarded a "Distinguished Service Award" on the merits of his generous community contributions for the city of Sacramento. He has chaired the Miss California Pageant, U.S.O., Red Cross, Cub Scouts, Salvation Army, Infantile Paralysis Ball, and the Under-privileged Childrens' Summer Camp Program, and is a trustee of the Boy Scouts of America.

When not traveling to a speaking engagement or selling financial programs, he can be found in Sacramento with his family; Norma, wife of 60 years, four sons, nine grandchildren, and two grandchildren.